Daily Mail
MONEY MAIL SAVERS' GUIDE

1997–98

Daily Mail

MONEY MAIL SAVERS' GUIDE

1997–98

ORION BUSINESS BOOKS

Copyright © Associated Newspapers Ltd 1997

All rights reserved

The right of Margaret Stone to be identified as the author of this work has been asserted by her in accordance with the Copyright, Designs and Patents Act, 1988

While every effort is made to ensure accuracy, the publishers, the editor, Associated Newspapers Ltd, their assigns, licensees and printers cannot accept any liability for any errors or omissions contained herein nor liability for any person acting or refraining from action as a result of the information contained in this book. The editor regrets that she cannot reply to personal tax problems.

First published in Great Britain in 1997 by
Orion Business
An imprint of the Orion Publishing Group Ltd
Orion House, 5 Upper St Martin's Lane, London WC2H 9EA

A CIP catalogue record for this book is available
from the British Library

ISBN 0-75280-529-0

Typeset by Selwood Systems, Midsomer Norton
Printed and bound in Great Britain by Butler & Tanner Ltd,
Frome and London

Contents

1. **Why Save?**   1
2. **From Safety First to High Risk**   9
3. **Tax and Savings**   12
4. **Capital Taxes**   16
5. **Tax Treatment of Your Investments**   20
6. **Savings and the Family**   24
7. **The Essential Savings**   26
8. **Savings Strategies**   29
9. **Investor Protection**   32
10. **High Street Banks**
    Children's Account   34
    Deposit Account   35
    High Interest Cheque Account   36
    Instant Access Account   38
    Interest-Bearing Current Account   39
    Monthly Income Account   40
    Notice Account   41
    SAYE – 2nd Issue   43
    SAYE – Series "F" Share Option Scheme   44
    Tax Exempt Special Savings Account (TESSA)   45
    Fixed Term Account   47
11. **Building Societies**
    Cash Card Account   49
    Current Account   50
    Children's Account   52
    Instant Access Account   53
    High Interest Cheque Account   55
    Monthly Income Account   56
    Notice Account   57
    Ordinary or Share Account   59
    Postal Account   60
    Regular Savings Account   62
    SAYE – 2nd Issue   63
    SAYE – Series "F" Share Option Scheme   64
    Tax Exempt Special Savings Account (TESSA)   66
    Fixed Term Share   67
12. **Gold**
    Gold Coins   69
13. **Friendly Society**
    Regular Savings Policy   71
14. **Life Insurance**
    Annuity   73
    Pension Annuity   74
    Flexible Annuity   76

CONTENTS

Distribution Bond — 77
Guaranteed Income and Growth Bonds — 79
Guaranteed Stock Market or Equity Bond — 80
High Income Bond — 82
Managed Bond — 83
School Fees Educational Trust — 85
Traded Endowment Policies — 86
Unit-Linked Regular Savings Plan — 87
With-Profits Endowment Policy — 89
With-Profits Flexible Policy — 90
With-Profit Bonds — 92
Temporary Annuity and "Back to Backs" — 93

15. Local Authorities
Local Authority Bond — 95
Negotiable or Yearling Bond — 96

16. National Savings
FIRST Option Bond — 98
Capital Bond – Series "J" — 99
Children's Bonus Bond – Issue "H" — 101
Deposit Bond — 102
Income Bond — 103
Investment Account — 104
Ordinary Account — 105
9th Issue Index-Linked Certificates — 107
43rd Issue Savings Certificates — 109
Pensioners Guaranteed Income Bond – Series "3" — 110
Premium Bond — 111
SAYE – 4th Issue Series "F" Share Option Scheme — 113
Yearly Plan — 114

17. Offshore Savings
Building Society Account — 115
Currency Fund — 117
High Interest Cheque Account — 118
Managed Currency Fund — 119
Fixed Rate Term Account — 121
Investment Funds — 122

18. Pensions
Additional Voluntary Contributions — 124
Personal Pension Plan — 126
Self-Employed Retirement Annuity — 127
Transfer Plan — 129

19. Shares
Business Expansion Scheme and Fund — 132
Enterprise Investment Scheme — 132
Investment Trusts — 134
Investment Trust Savings Scheme — 135
Ordinary Quoted — 137
Personal Equity Plan — 139
Permanent Interest Bearing Shares — 140
Shares on the Alternative Investment Market — 142
Unit Trust — 143
Unit Trust or Investment Trust PEP — 146
Unit Trust Savings Scheme — 147
Venture Capital Trust — 148

20. Stocks
Bond Fund — 151
Government Index-Linked — 152
Government Stock — 154
Loan and Debenture (Corporate Bonds) — 156

Appendix 1
Shareholder Perks — 158

Appendix 2
Recent Issues of National Savings Certificates — 170
General Extension Rates: Interest Variable — 178
Older Issues of National Savings Certificates — 178

Appendix 3
The Retail Prices Index — 179
Index-Linked Savings Certificates — 179

Appendix 4
CAR – The Real Rate of Interest — 181
Gross and Net Interest Rates — 182

Index — 183

CHAPTER 1

Why Save?

Nearly everyone saves at some point in his or her life if only for fairly obvious reasons, such as a deposit for a house, paying for a daughter's wedding or a new car.

Other people, even if they have no particular objective in mind, have a more or less continuous savings programme setting money aside on either a regular or more intermittent basis.

The Victorians identified it as the virtue thrift and although the nineteenth century connotations no longer apply – we don't need the protection of savings to avoid, at all costs, the fate of the workhouse – saving is still a good habit to acquire.

In the broadest possible terms, the money will always come in handy and, more importantly, it is a failsafe – should an emergency or personal disaster occur. Saving cannot prevent either happening, but it can alleviate some of the worst side effects.

But a vague appreciation that savings are "a good thing" is not really enough. To make the most of the very many different forms of savings and investment that are available, you do some preliminary fact-finding – about you.

For example, do you know exactly what your income is, let alone your after tax income? Do you know how much income you can expect in retirement? Are you panic-stricken at the thought of investment losing value? Do you even know what you want from your savings? Many people, it must be admitted, are a little woolly about the financial facts of life.

To help you decide (a) what you need from your savings and (b) the strategy to help you obtain it, answer the following basic questions.

Can I afford to save?

If the answer to this question and the next four questions is "No", then you have problems. Some, such as long term unemployment where savings can almost be a positive disadvantage, may be intractable. (Income Support is only available in full for those with savings of £3,000 or less, with scaled down benefits for those with savings up to £8,000. For housing benefit, council tax benefit and long-term care the ceiling is £16,000 with the first £10,000 completely ignored.) Others may be just a matter of making life-style adjustments.

Use the family budget planner on page 3 to work out just exactly where your disposable income goes. There are some interesting cost comparisons per month on page 4. Each individual and family must decide their own priorities, but it is important that you can answer "yes" to the next four questions.

Have I "rainy day" or emergency savings?

Advance notice is not given for most emergencies: the car clutch goes; the cistern bursts or a close member of your family working abroad becomes seriously ill. Can you afford the costs involved?

Before you begin any fancy footwork with exciting new investments such as new share issues, or even opt for higher interest on savings locked away for a longer time, make sure you have sufficient savings which are *immediately* available (or at the most can be withdrawn within two days).

The amount you need to save will vary from individual to individual, family to family. It should be £100–£300 at the very least and £500 is not too much for a single person. Married couples should think in terms of £1,000–£2,000 minimum. See Chapter Seven for more detailed analysis of suitable rainy day savings.

Will my family be financially protected should I die or be permanently unable to work?

Mortgage payments, HP commitments, food costs, electricity bills and school fees (to mention but a few of the family's outgoings) won't stop if you die.

Life assurance is the principal means of making sure that your family or other dependants, such as elderly parents, will have financial security in the event of your death.

The cheapest form of life assurance, a good value-for-money buy, is *term assurance* – however, it is not included here because it has no investment content. It pays out only in the event of the policyholder's death. The cost is around £18.00 a month for a 30-year-old man wanting £100,000 of cover for 20 years. Nor are the policies which cover you against sickness or accident included here.

- How much life insurance cover? As a very rough guide, think in terms of up to five times earnings. But don't forget that if you have

- *An endowment mortgage* – this should repay the house loan
- Or belong to a *company pension scheme* – you might have death cover up to four times salary built into the scheme. But remember, should you leave the pension scheme that benefit will disappear, unless you join a similar scheme.

Am I satisfied with my present living accommodation?

If you are renting a flat or house, or sharing with your parents, the answer will probably be "No". In which case you need to start saving, hard, for your own home, and to get your feet on the housing ladder. It is sometimes possible to obtain 100 per cent home loans, but it is still wise to save (see Chapter Seven).

- It will get you in the habit of setting aside a large sum each month; otherwise you might find these monthly mortgage payments a bit of a shock.
- If you have a deposit, you might not have to pay the one-off premium of a mortgage guarantee insurance policy which lenders require on loans above 70–85 per cent of the house price.
- Legal fees, moving expenses and furnishings will eat into any savings, even if you don't need or wish for a deposit.

Am I saving enough for my retirement?

To a certain extent *all* of your savings can be described, ultimately, as being for your retirement.

But there will be many other calls and temptations on your funds between now and then, so it is important to have some savings and investments which are not only specifically earmarked for retirement, but cannot be taken except as a pension.

Chapter Seven looks at this subject in more detail; and at the ways of improving your retirement income if you feel that, hitherto, you have been a little lax in respect of this essential saving.

WHY SAVE?

OUTGOINGS PER MONTH
Unavoidable expenditure

FOOD . . . . . £ ———

HOUSING

Mortgage/rent . . . £ ———

Ground rent . . . . £ ———

Water rates . . . . £ ———

Council tax . . . . £ ———

HEATING

Electricity . . . . £ ———

Gas . . . . . £ ———

Other fuel etc. . . . £ ———

INSURANCE

Contents . . . . £ ———

Building . . . . . £ ———

Life assurance . . . £ ———

Motor . . . . . £ ———

Mortgage protection . . £ ———

Other . . . . . £ ———

Pension contributions . . £ ———

TRAVEL

Season ticket . . . £ ———

Car tax . . . . £ ———

Maintenance payments . . £ ———

Child care . . . . £ ———

Other . . . . . £ ———

TOTAL   £ ———

SAVINGS

PAY council tax and water rates by instalments. PAY bills together through Giro to save postage and bank charges. PAY car tax for the full year. COMBINED house and buildings insurance can be cheaper. BUY the longest season ticket possible. INSULATE the house for substantial saving on energy bills. TURNING down the thermostat 4°F can save 10 per cent on heating bills. CHECK out school shops for second-hand school clothes. BUY own brand food.

TAX TIPS

KEEP mortgage to £30,000 for maximum tax relief. BE wary of switching to another lender if your existing mortgage covers home improvements made before 6 April 1988. You could lose tax relief on this part of the new loan. CHECK your PAYE notice of coding (sent in January and February) to make sure all the allowances to which you are entitled are there. HIGHER rate taxpayers and people with income from other sources should check their Schedule E Notice of Assessment which explains how the Revenue has worked out your tax bill. If you disagree, appeal within 30 days.

DON'TS

DON'T buy gas, electricity or telephone stamps, but put money into a building society. DON'T pay for gas or electricity through a slot meter. DON'T heat unused rooms. DON'T over-insure. DON'T cash in a life insurance policy early; surrender values are poor. DON'T cash in any life insurance bought before March 1984; you will lose valuable tax relief. NEVER pay in advance if you can pay in arrears.

WHY SAVE?

	Cost per month
Twenty filter-tip cigarettes a day at £3.00 a pack	£84.00
Shampoo and blow dry at £9 a week	£36.00
Two pints of beer a day at £1.80 a pint	£108.00
Cat food at £2.80 a week	£11.20
Two weekly magazines at 50p per week	£4.00
Pocket money for 14–16-year-olds at £3.60 per week (TSB pocket money survey)	£14.40
Mortgage protection plan for 25 years for a 35-year-old man per £50,000 house loan	£7.75
Unit trust monthly savings plan	£30.00
Minimum holding in National Savings Certificates	£100
Minimum monthly savings – Personal Equity Plan	£25–£30
Some bank and building society accounts can still be opened for as little as	£1–£5

Additional checks

Life assurance

If you really do have life policies which are surplus to requirements and need to cash them in (rather than making them "paid up"), you will get more money from selling the policies than surrendering them. There is a brisk market in second-hand policies. The Association of Policy Market Makers (0171–739 3949) will provide a list of companies which deal in second-hand policies.

Direct Debits

Electricity Companies – Incentive schemes for direct debit payments*

Eastern Electricity:	2% off unit & standing charge
East Midlands Electicity:	£5 pa discount
London Electricity	4% off annual bill
MANWEB:	£1 pq off service charge & 1.5% off the unit charge
Midlands Electricity:	6.84p + VAT per unit – direct debit 7.017p + VAT per unit – otherwise
NORWEB:	c 2% off unit rate and standing charge
Northern Electric:	1%, guaranteed – going up to a minimum of £3 pa.
Scottish Power:	£4 pa.
Scottish Hydro:	2% off unit rate, 4% from April
Seeboard:	£1 pq.
Southern Electric:	1.25% off unit rate
S. Western Electricity	2% off bill
S. Wales Electricity:	2.5% off unit price, £1.20 off standing charge
Yorkshire Electricity:	£10 pa.

Source: Direct Debit.

*Correct at January 1997.

OUTGOINGS PER MONTH
Other essentials

Petrol
Other fares . . . . £_____
TV licence . . . . £_____
School fees/
   clothes . . . . £_____
Telephone . . . . £_____
Garage repairs . . . £_____
Medical/Dentist . . . £_____

LOANS
HP . . . . . £_____
Personal loan . . . . £_____
Overdraft . . . . £_____

TOTAL £_____

WHY SAVE?

SAVINGS

TELEPHONE during cheap rate periods. CONSIDER using another telecom supplier, particularly if you make frequent overseas calls. PAY regular bills by standing order, better still direct debit, to save postage. SEARCH out interest-free credit offers. An OVERDRAFT is cheaper than a personal loan if you can get one. DRIVE carefully to conserve petrol. CONVERT your car to unleaded petrol, it's cheaper. PAY school fees in advance: can be 40 per cent cheaper. ALWAYS check for hidden charges in any credit deal. CHECK bank statements thoroughly. LIMIT directory enquiry calls (now 25p for maximum two enquiries). CONVERT your current account to one which pays interest.

TAX TIPS

TAKE out as large a pension as you can afford. A pension-linked mortgage, with tax relief at 15 per cent on the mortgage interest (up to £30,000 of loan) and pension contributions, is very tax efficient. MARRIED couples should make sure that the wife's personal tax allowances of £4,045 (from 6 April 1997) is used. Transfer savings from joint accounts to her name to maximise the family's tax free income and capital gains tax allowances.

DON'TS

DON'T borrow money to pay off debts. DON'T go into the red without consulting your bank manager; bank charges on unauthorised borrowings are high. BANK budget accounts cost a lot; organise your own system. DON'T spend money wrongly credited to your account; it has to go back. DON'T raise a loan on trading cheques; rates are astronomical.

Overdraft interest

Your bank manager will almost invariably suggest a bank personal loan – which costs more than an overdraft. What is more, the interest rate is fixed for the duration of the loan, irrespective of what might happen to interest rates. Discuss your credit arrangements with him/her. Most managers will probably accede to your request for an overdraft although you will probably have to pay an arrangement fee. Then negotiate for the interest rate: overdraft rates range from 2½ per cent to 6 per cent over bank base rates. Most customers will be fobbed off with 5 per cent: persuade your bank manager to go lower. Check if your bank operates a "buffer zone" which allows you to go modestly in the red without charge.

OUTGOINGS PER MONTH
Important costs

HOUSEHOLD

Kitchen equipment	£_____
Cleaning and toiletries	£_____
Hairdressing	£_____
Decorating	£_____
Birthday, Xmas presents	£_____
Holidays	£_____
Evening classes	£_____
Pocket money	£_____
Garden tools	£_____
Trade union fees	£_____
Vet	£_____
TV rental	£_____
School trips	£_____
Other	£_____
TOTAL	£_____

One of the cheapest forms of overdraft credit is available to holders of "Gold" cards – the up-market charge or credit cards which have a built-in automatic overdraft facility up to £10,000, by negotiation.

SAVINGS

BUY in bulk if there is room for storage. SEARCH out grants wherever these might be available; they are free gifts. CHECK your credit card terms: balance a flat initial fee with a lower interest rate (suitable if you use the credit regularly) against no fee and a higher interest rate. INSURE pets when they are young to cover later vet's bills. SOME subscriptions offer discount for paying by direct debit. USE customer discount cards where available.

TAX TIPS

USE child's tax relief allowance wherever possible; have money gifts made direct to a child. CHILDREN can earn up to £4,045 a year before paying tax. Be careful about putting money such as Child Benefit payments, direct into a savings account in the child's name. Interest over £100 on children's savings given by parents, is taxed as though it belongs to the parents!

DON'TS

DON'T rent household equipment, televisions, video recorders and compact disc players; it's cheaper to buy. This includes telephones, but make sure you buy one that has been approved for connection to British Telecom lines – it will carry a green circle.

Pensions 1:

Many self-employed are wary about tying up the maximum possible into their private pension arrangements despite the attractive element of tax relief built into such schemes. Pension fund monies cannot be released (as a pension or permitted cash commutation) until stated retirement age. However, it is always possible to activate the pension plan "loan back" arrangements should an urgent need for cash emerge in the meantime.

OUTGOINGS PER MONTH
Flexible costs

Clothes	£_____
Furnishing	£_____
Magazines and newspapers	£_____
Cosmetics	£_____
Postage and stationery	£_____
Garden	£_____
Laundry	£_____
Xmas entertainment	£_____
Credit cards	£_____
Savings	£_____
TOTAL	£_____

Pensions 2:

Anyone not belonging to a company pension scheme can get tax relief up to 17.5 per cent of net relevant earnings (more once you are 36). If you haven't paid the maximum allowed in any of the previous six tax years, you can top up those contributions and obtain tax relief for those years.

WHY SAVE?

Pensions 3:

At retirement, remember that you can shop around to obtain a better annuity rate than that offered by the company with which you took out a personal pension plan. You are able to defer buying an annuity for up to five years – useful if your retirement date coincides with a period when annuity rates are low.

DON'TS

DON'T buy clothes that can't go in the washing machine; dry cleaning costs are high. LEARN a money-making skill at evening classes. SHOP at sale times. ASK for discount for cash wherever appropriate.

Direct debits

Some subscriptions are cheaper if you pay by direct debit. Most electricity companies offer a discount to customers paying this way (see page 4). You might also save money if payments are debited from your bank account this way rather than by paying for the bills with more expensive-to-handle (from the bank's point of view) cheques, as some banks still charge more for cheque withdrawals. Of course, this charge only applies if your account is not in credit – free banking, although not universally available, with the majority of bank accounts applies when the account is in the black.

SAVINGS

DUAL pricing is now allowed; pay by cash if it is cheaper than using a credit card. PAY credit card bill in full every month to avoid interest charges; some cards now charge interest from the purchase date if the account is not cleared that month. AVOID store cards which usually have a higher interest rate than bank credit cards. PAY store cards, if you insist on using them, by direct debit if you can't repay in full, as the interest charge is often lower. This is the case with some credit cards too.

TAX TIPS

HIGHER rate taxpayers should look for tax-free investments such as National Savings Certificates, Tessas and PEPs (see individual sections for details). NON-taxpayers should go for investments that pay interest gross and register to receive interest without deduction of tax (otherwise it will be paid and a time interval will occur before the tax can be reclaimed). A wife's investment income can now be offset against her personal tax allowance, so a non-working wife's savings should be in gross-paying investments to "use up" her personal allowance. Since April 1991 banks and building societies have been able to pay interest gross to non-taxpayers.

OUTGOINGS PER MONTH
Desirable costs

Charity donations	£_____
Eating out	£_____
Cinema and theatre	£_____
Alcohol and tobacco . . .	£_____
Hobbies/sport	£_____
Toys	£_____
Books	£_____
Records/tapes	£_____
Gambling	£_____
Office collections . . .	£_____
TOTAL	£_____

SAVINGS

SOME theatres and cinemas sell half-price seats on Mondays. MATINEE performances are cheaper and less crowded. PENSIONER price concessions are often available. SET menus offer far better value than à la carte. WATCH out for special promotion offers for eating out and travel.

TAX TIPS

MAKE charitable donations under covenant or the gift aid scheme (for lump sums) for tax advantage. CONSIDER using a credit card which makes donations to named charities related to the amount cardholders spend. GAMBLING and National Lottery winnings are tax free.

DON'TS

DON'T sell any valuables to doorstep hawkers; get comparative valuations. DON'T spend needlessly on children.

Company loans

Cheap or interest-free company loans, for example, to buy an expensive season ticket could result in a higher tax bill. The Inland Revenue counts it as a taxable benefit, assessing the value according to the "official rate of interest" applied to the loan.

Provided the loan does not exceed £5,000, no tax will be charged.

Consolidation loans

It is tempting to take out a consolidation loan to take care of all existing debts, but many debts – such as gas, electricity and telephone bills – are renewed every few months. As a rule of thumb, the borrowing term should not exceed the life span of the asset you are buying. For example, cars are renewed every two to three years; holidays come round once a year; electricity and other service bills once a quarter. Tailor your borrowing accordingly so that you have repaid one loan before the next one is taken out.

Interest-free credit

Although this is valuable, do make sure that the store or shop which is offering it is not charging a price at the upper end of the scale. With hi-fi and some "white" goods, the prices in discount stores might be sufficiently attractive to outweigh a temporary interest charge or loss of interest if you mobilise savings to buy them. Shopping around can be both tedious, time-consuming and only marginally beneficial: sometimes – and with these kind of goods in particular – it can be very worthwhile.

Rented equipment

If you still prefer to rent your TV and similar equipment, keep an eye on the tariff and standard of equipment currently offered by the renter. You might be paying a rate, fixed some time ago, on equipment which is now let for a lower rental, or could "swap" your CD and video recorder, say, for a more comprehensive system for the same price.

CHAPTER 2

From Safety First to High Risk

The difference between savings and investment is that the former is safer than investment which will always involve some element of risk. Understanding the risk spectrum from "safety first" to "high risk" is an important aspect of managing one's money well and deciding the most appropriate savings strategy (see Chapter Eight).

To help readers of *Money Mail Savers' Guide* we have devised a ratings guide which identifies the degree of investment risk that different kinds of savings and investment have.

Money Mail Rating

Safe *****
Sound ****!
Opportunity **!!!
Aggressive *!!!!
Risky !!!!!

It is an at-a-glance ratings symbol which gives readers a quick guide to the kind of investment they might be contemplating. The second half of this book, which goes through each investment one-by-one, uses this rating.

The qualities which determine an investment's risk are whether the capital value is fixed or varies; whether the rate of interest is fixed; the currency; whether the investment is narrowly or widely spread; and the market for those investments.

So the spectrum ranges from National Savings Certificates to unquoted foreign companies.

The various investment categories are:

- Fixed capital, fixed interest
- Fixed capital, variable interest
- Variable capital, fixed interest
- Variable capital, variable interest
- Variable capital, variable interest, variable currency
- Variable capital, no interest

Fixed capital, fixed interest

This type of investment is the safest of all. The investor knows, at any time, exactly what he will obtain from his money.

In this category are:
Bank, Deposit Taker and Offshore
　Term Accounts
　Tax Exempt Special Savings Accounts
Life Insurance
　Guaranteed Growth & Income Bonds – provided they are held to maturity
　Annuity

Local Authority
  Loans
  Corporation Stock ⎱ provided they are held
  Yearling Bond ⎰ to maturity
National Savings
  Capital Bonds
  First Option Bond
  Pensioners Guaranteed Income Bond
  43rd Issue National Savings Certificates
Stock
  Government fixed interest – provided held to maturity
Money Mail Rating *****

Fixed capital, variable interest

This form of investment is very safe, because the investor can always get his original capital back in full, even though the rate of interest it earns may vary.
In this category are:
Banks
  Deposit Account
  Children's Account
  High Interest Cheque Account
  High Interest Deposit Account
  Monthly Savings Account
  Notice Account
  Offshore High Interest Cheque Account
  Tax Exempt Special Savings Account
Building Society
  Cash Card Account
  Cheque Book Account
  Children's Account
  Instant Access Account
  Monthly Income
  Monthly Savings Account
  Notice Account
  Offshore Share Account
  Tax Exempt Special Savings Account
  Term Share
Life Insurance
  With-Profits Endowment – provided they are held to maturity
  With-Profits Flexible Endowment – provided they are held to guaranteed surrender dates
National Savings
  Income Bonds
  Investment Account
  Ordinary Account
  Index-Linked Certificates
  Premium Bonds
Pensions
  Additional Voluntary Contributions
  Transfer Plan
Money Mail Rating *****

Variable capital, fixed interest

Such investment is moving out of the very safe category. Although the interest remains fixed, there can be wide fluctuations in capital values, leaving the investor hopefully better off, but maybe worse off. These investments are therefore not suitable for emergency funds. In this category are:
Variable capital, fixed
  Government and Local Authority Stock – unless held to redemption
  Company Loan and Debenture Stock – unless held to redemption
  Preference Shares
Money Mail Rating ****! *to* **!!!

Variable capital, variable interest

This covers a very wide range of share investments, with different degrees of risk which depend upon the size, track record and marketability of individual shares in different companies, and whether or not the investment is widely spread, to narrow the risk over the range of shares. But they are all risky investments in which an investor can see his capital dwindle, occasionally disappear, and his income suffer the same fate.
Shares
  Companies listed on the Stock Exchange, including those held in Personal Equity Plans.

Smaller and younger companies with shares quoted on the Alternative Investment Market.
Money Mail Rating **!!! *to* !!!!!
Investment Trusts
　including Personal Equity Plans
Unit Trusts
　including Personal Equity Plans
Money Mail Rating ****! *to* *!!!!
Life Assurance
　Friendly Society Savings Plan
　Investment Bonds
　Unit-Linked Savings
Money Mail Rating ****! *to* *!!!!

Variable capital, variable interest, variable currency

Currencies rise and fall in value against each other, and investments which have to get the currency right as well as the underlying investments have a very high risk factor. Investment managers admit that selecting the right currency and "hedging" (to minimise the risk) is one of their most difficult tasks.
Offshore
　Currency Funds
　Unit Trusts
Money Mail Rating **!!! *to* !!!!!

Variable capital, no interest

Investments such as commodities, precious metals, antiques which may not be easily marketable
Gold
Offshore funds investing in alternative investments
Money Mail Rating *!!!! *to* !!!!!

CHAPTER 3

Tax and Savings

If the most fundamental reasons for saving are *emergencies, family protection, house purchase* and *provision for old age*, the most significant feature underlying your savings and investment decisions after assessing the *risk factor* is *tax*, which affects the return you get on your investments.

Some forms of investment and savings are more suitable for higher rate taxpayers; others will be of more benefit to those who pay little or no tax.

The first income tax band is 20 per cent (levied on taxable income up to £4,100). Then both income and capital gains are now taxed at the same rates: either 25 per cent or 40 per cent. Capital gains tax liabilities sit on top of income, and could push you into the 40 per cent bracket if your *total* taxable income plus taxable gains exceeds £26,100.

To make the most of the wide variety of savings discussed in greater detail later, it is sensible to get to grips with the tax system and how it affects you and your family.

Since 6 April 1996 all savings interest and dividend income has tax deducted at the savings rate of 20 per cent. This benefits 23 per cent basic rate taxpayers who gain 3 per cent "more" from this interest. It makes life simpler for 20 per cent taxpayers who no longer have to reclaim the extra 3 per cent deducted. Higher rate taxpayers, however, must pay the difference of 20 per cent to bring tax they pay up to 40 per cent.

Income tax

Contrary to general myth we don't pay tax on all our income. Everyone, from the youngest baby in the country to the oldest pensioner, is entitled to some tax-free income (assuming, of course, that they have some income). In addition, some state benefits are tax free, some expenditure is given tax relief and the interest on certain forms of savings is tax free.

The principal tax-free *allowances* vary according to marital status and age, and whether you are a single-parent family (see tax table on page **14**).

Certain outgoings are given tax relief up to a certain amount. These include:

- Mortgage interest relief at 15 per cent rate of tax only on home loans up to £30,000.
- Pension scheme contributions of up to 15 per cent of your earnings if employed, or 17½ per cent if self-employed or not in a company pension scheme, rising with a personal pension plan to 20 per cent at age 36 and increasing to a maximum of 40 per cent at age 61 and over, qualify for tax relief at your top rate of tax. (From age 36 contributions are less generous for the old-style retirement annuities.) Members of company pension schemes who joined after 1 June 1989 will be restricted to tax relief on pension scheme contributions on earnings up to £84,000 only.

TAX AND SAVINGS

The same limits apply to personal pension plans taken out since 6 April 1989.
- Maintenance and alimony payments made before 15 March 1988 are given tax relief; on agreements made from 15 March 1988 relief is given up to a limit equal to the difference between the single and married person's allowance.
- Covenanted payments to charities attract tax relief at basic and higher rate tax.
- Life assurance policies taken out before 13 March 1984 qualify for tax relief at 12½ per cent.
- Payroll deductions to charity up to a maximum donation of £100 a month qualify for tax relief.
- Individual gifts to charity over £250 (net) are tax free. Gifts are paid net of basic rate tax; higher rate tax relief is claimed by the taxpayer.

Income and savings which are exempt from income tax are:

- National Savings Bank Ordinary Account – the first £70 of interest a year. (£140 in a joint account.)
- National Savings Certificates (index-linked as well as conventional).
- National Savings Yearly Plan – the interest. †
- Premium Bond prizes.
- Save As You Earn (SAYE) bonuses. †
- Personal Equity Plan – dividends, whether they are reinvested or distributed.
- Tax Exempt Special Savings Account (Tessa) – tax free if held for five years; if income is withdrawn earlier it is paid net; the tax withheld is paid as a tax-free bonus after five years.
- Life assurance policies – the proceeds of qualifying policies (usually where regular payments are in force) paid out either at death or after 7½–10 years.
- Annuities – a proportion of the annuity income which varies with age. This does not apply to pension annuities which are taxable as income.
- Football pools – the winnings; and other betting winnings (although you may have to pay betting tax).
- Maintenance payments – on agreements made from 15 March 1988.
- Redundancy payments – up to £30,000.
- Rental income up to £4,250 from letting a room(s) in your home.

† These have been withdrawn for new customers but tax free benefits still apply to existing holders.

Benefits which are not taxable and which should not be entered on your tax return include:
Child benefit
Mobility allowance
One-parent benefit
Guardian's allowance and child's special allowance
Income support
Industrial disablement benefits
Severe disablement allowance
Christmas bonus paid with state pension or allowance
Child dependency additions
Family credit
Short-Term Incapacity Benefit
Housing benefit
Attendance allowance
Social fund payments
Maternity allowance
Invalidity benefit
Widow's payment

Pensions which are non-taxable and should not be entered on your tax return include:
War widows' pension.
Certain pensions for wounds or disability caused or aggravated by military service or for other war injuries.
Pensions paid to victims of Nazi persecution by the German or Austrian governments should be entered, although special provisions apply.

Grants which are non-taxable and should not be entered on your tax return include:
Assisted places grant
Student grant

Working out your tax bill

Basic rate is only levied on your *taxable income*: this is your income after deducting your allowances and permitted outgoings and ignoring, of course, tax-free income.

TAX AND SAVINGS

Income Tax Rates

Taxable Income		Rate	Tax payable
	£	%	£
1997–98	0– 4,100	20	820
	4,101–26,100	23	5,060
	over 26,100	40	
1996–97	0– 3,900	20	780
	3,901–25,500	24	5,184
	over 25,500	40	
	1997–98	1995–96	1995–96
Additional rate (discretionary trusts)		10	10

Income Tax allowances

	1997–98	1996–97
	£	£
Personal	4,045	3,765
Married couple*	1,830#	1,790#
Additional personal and widow's bereavement	1,830#	1,790#
Personal (65–74)	5,220	4,910
Married couple (65–74)*	3,185#	3,115#
Personal (75 plus)	5,400	5,090
Married couple (75 plus)*	3,225#	3,155#
Blind person's**	1,280	1,250
Age allowance income limit†	15,600	15,200
Rent a room	4,250	3,250

* This is in addition to the personal allowance which *each* spouse receives; in the first instance it is given to the husband.

\# At lower 15 per cent rate only.

** Reduced by any tax-free disability benefit received.

† Once income exceeds £15,600 the age allowance is reduced by £1 for every £2 of income until it reaches the level of the normal allowances. The extra personal allowance runs out at £17,950 (age 65–74) or £18,310 (75 plus); for the partner claiming the married couple's allowance at £20,660 (65–74) or £21,100 (75 plus).

There is a reduced rate band of 20 per cent on the first £4,100 of income. Basic rate tax is currently 23 per cent on taxable income between £4,101 and £26,100; anything over that is taxed at 40 per cent.

There are 25 million taxpayers, of whom 2,400,000 pay higher rate tax.

Pensioners who are reliant on the state retirement pension only are unlikely to be taxpayers, but need to be very careful that modest savings which are taxed at source don't tip them into the basic rate tax bracket (see Chapter Five).

Trust income

Using trusts for both convenience and tax planning has a long history. There are basically three kinds of trust: income in possession trusts, discretionary trusts, and accumulation and maintenance trusts.

Interest in possession trusts, which give the beneficiary the right to the trust income, are widely used for inheritance tax planning as the lifetime gift to the trust is a PET – that is a Potentially Exempt Transfer. Provided the settlor survives seven years after making the gift, it will pass beyond the inheritance tax net (see page **18**). The beneficiary pays income tax at his or her appropriate tax rate.

The beneficiary of a discretionary trust does not have the automatic right to income; as the name indicates, it is at the discretion of the trustees. This affects the tax treatment of the income. There is a special rate of tax for discretionary trusts which is basic rate tax (23 per cent) plus an additional rate (10 per cent), making a combined total of 33 per cent.

If the income is distributed to a child or other non-taxpayer, the 33 per cent tax paid can be reclaimed. With a child, use tax form R40 to reclaim the tax. However, if the parent has settled the gift, the child's trust income will be aggregated with his own.

Accumulation and maintenance trusts, used often to provide school fees, work in a similar way. It is quite possible that the income will not be distributed immediately, in which case the trustees will pay the 33 per cent tax on the trust fund's income. This can then be paid out later as capital without a further charge to tax.

The big difference between discretionary trusts and accumulation and maintenance trusts is in respect of inheritance tax. Gifts into the former are not PETs, but are subject to inheritance tax at the reduced lifetime rate of 20 per cent. Gifts into the latter trust, provided the settlor survives seven years, are exempt from inheritance tax.

Trusts are very useful for helping with estate and tax planning where substantial sums are involved. It costs £300–£500 to set up a trust.

CHAPTER 4

Capital Taxes

Income tax isn't the only tax you must consider; the capital taxes – capital gains tax and inheritance tax (formerly capital transfer tax) – can have some bearing on your investment decisions.

Capital gains tax

If you make a profit when you sell an asset (or indeed give it away for more than its acquisition value) then you have made a capital gain. Conversely, you might have a capital loss on your hands if the asset has decreased in value before you sell or part with it.

In each tax year capital gains, less capital losses and any expenses incurred in buying and selling (such as legal fees or commission), are, if they exceed a certain level, subject to capital gains tax at either 23 per cent or 40 per cent. Your taxable gains are aggregated with your income to determine which rate you pay (see Chapter Three).

There are several comforting facts to remember about capital gains tax.

- Many types of assets are exempt from capital gains tax.
- Capital gains tax only applies to the *gains* you make, not the actual disposal price.
- The level at which the tax begins is sufficiently high – £6,500 in tax year 1997–98 – to keep many investors out of this tax net.
- Only gains accrued since 31 March 1982 will be taxable.
- The indexation of capital gains made since March 1982, which "increases" the purchase price of your asset in line with the rise in the retail price index, makes it even less likely that capital gains tax will apply.
- Capital losses can be offset against taxable gains, but can also, if not used in one tax year, be carried forward indefinitely to set against capital gains you might make in the future. However, losses on disposals made after 29 November 1994 cannot be increased in line with indexation.
- No capital gains tax is paid at death: whoever inherits your assets does so at the market value at your death.
- Retirement relief from age 50 (55 before 28 November 1995) benefits business owners. The first 100 per cent of the gain is tax free up to £250,000; on the next £750,000, 50 per cent is tax free.

Principal assets exempt from capital gains tax

You will not have to pay capital gains tax on the disposal of the following assets:

Your principal home If you have more than one house you can select which is your main home provided the choice is made within three years of buying the second. You can subsequently change your mind, but can only back-date your choice by two years.

Your car

Your "chattels" – personal belongings such as furniture and jewellery sold for £6,500 or less; gallantry decorations you have earned, not bought, are totally exempt.

National Savings Certificates, Yearly Plan, Capital Bond, First Option Bond, Pensioners Guaranteed Income Bond, Save As You Earn (SAYE) and Premium Bond prizes.

British Government stock and company loan or debenture stock.

Legal tender (which still includes gold sovereigns, half sovereigns and the Britannia gold coins) and any foreign currency obtained for personal use abroad.

Personal Equity Plan

Tax Exempt Special Savings Accounts

Business Expansion Scheme shares held for qualifying five years.

Enterprise Investment Scheme shares held for qualifying five years.

Venture Capital Trust shares held for the qualifying five years.

Tangible movable property with a predictable life of no more than 50 years such as boats, caravans and animals.

Life insurance policies of which you are the original owner.

Gifts to charities or the nation.

Indexation of capital gains

Inflation, as opposed to real growth in the value of any assets you subsequently sell, is taken into account by linking the purchase price with the change in the Retail Price Index since then.

This has the effect of "increasing" the purchase price and thereby reducing or even eliminating your capital gain altogether. In the latter case, it has actually created a capital loss.

On post 31 March 1982 gains, use the Retail Price Index for the appropriate month (see page **180**) to work out the index-linked value which is to be added to your original purchase price.

For example, take shares bought in August 1984 for £3,000 and sold for £6,000 in January 1987. The Retail Price Index rose by 10.8 per cent between August 1984 and December 1986. As 10.8 per cent of £3,000 is £324, that amount of index-linked value must be added to your original purchase price of £3,000, bringing it to £3,324 and thus reducing the capital gain to £2,676. Losses made on disposals after 29 November 1994 cannot be increased in line with indexation.

Inheritance tax

Inheritance tax replaced capital transfer tax on 18 March 1986. It bears more resemblance to the old estate duty (which was itself replaced by capital transfer tax) in that only gifts at death (or near) are taxable.

Substantial exemptions from inheritance tax are allowed and in addition the first £215,000 of gifts or bequests is also exempt from the tax. The balance attracts tax at 40 per cent (other than lifetime gifts to discretionary trusts where the rate is 20 per cent).

However, substantial house price inflation means that many people who might hitherto have considered they had "little to leave" might find their estate liable to this tax.

All gifts made seven years before death are tax free. All non-exempt gifts made within three years of death are liable to inheritance tax and included in your estate. Gifts made between three and seven years are taxed on a sliding scale.

Inheritance tax rates from 6 April 1997

Portion of value £,000	On death* Rate of Tax
0–215	Nil
Over 215	40%

Inheritance tax rates from 6 April 1996

Portion of value £,000	On death* Rate of tax
0–200	Nil
Over 200	40%

* Also applies to any gift made within three years of death.

Gifts exempt from inheritance tax

- Gifts between husband and wife.
- Gifts of £3,000 in each tax year; an unused portion can be brought forward one year.
- Wedding gifts: parents – £5,000 each; grandparents, great-grandparents and bride and groom to each other – £2,500; anyone else – £1,000.
- Any number of individual gifts not exceeding £250 (provided the recipient has not received gifts under the two previous headings).
- Money spent on your child's maintenance and education; reasonable provision for care of dependent relative.
- "Normal expenditure" gifts out of taxed income (*not* capital), the making of which does not affect your standard of living.
- Gifts to charities.
- Gifts to museums, art galleries and the National Trust including property of "outstanding national interest".

Gifts made within seven years of death – Reduced tax charge

	% of death charge
more than seven years before	0
more than six years before	20
more than five years before	40
more than four years before	60
more than three years before	80
less than three years before	100

CAPITAL TAXES

Free tax leaflets from the Inland Revenue*

Booklet no.	Title	Booklet no.	Title
IR1	Extra-statutory concessions	IR86	A Guide to Mortgage Interest for Married Couples
IR4	Income tax and Pensioners		
IR4A	Income Tax – Age Allowance	IR87	Rooms To Let
IR11	Tax Treatment of Interest Paid	IR89	Personal Equity Plans (PEPs)
IR13	Income Tax – Wife's Earnings Election	IR90	Independent Taxation – A Guide to Tax Allowances and Reliefs
IR20	Residents and Non-Residents – Liability to tax in the UK	IR91	A Guide for Widows and Widowers
		IR92	Income Tax – A Guide for One-parent Families
IR22	Income Tax – Personal Allowances		
IR23	Income Tax and Widows	IR93	Separation, Divorce and Maintenance Payments
IR24	Class 4 National Insurance Contributions	IR95	Shares for Employees – Profit Sharing Schemes
IR28	Starting in Business		
IR33	Income Tax and School Leavers	IR97	Shares for Employees – SAYE Share Options
IR34	Income Tax – Pay As You Earn		
IR41	Income Tax and the Unemployed	IR103	Tax Relief for Private Medical Insurance
IR42	Income Tax – Lay-offs and short time work		
		IR110	Can you stop paying tax on your bank and building society interest?
IR43	Income Tax and Strikes		
IR45	Income Tax, Capital Gains Tax and Capital Transfer Tax – What happens when someone dies	IR111	How to claim a repayment of tax on bank and building society interest
		IR112	How to claim a repayment of income tax
IR46	Income Tax and Corporation Tax – Clubs, Societies and Associations		
		IR113	Gift Aid – A Guide for Donors and Charities
IR51	Business Expansion Scheme		
IR52	Your Tax Office – why it is where it is	IR114	TESSA – Tax Free Interest for Taxpayers
IR56/N139	Employed or Self-Employed?	IR115	Tax and Childcare
IR57	Thinking of working for yourself?	IR121	Income Tax and Pensioners
IR58	Going to Work Abroad?	CGT	Capital Gains Tax – An Introduction
IR60	Income Tax and Students		
IR63	MIRAS Mortgage Interest Relief at Source	CGT4	Capital Gains Tax – Owner-occupied Houses
IR65	Giving to Charity – how individuals can get tax relief	CGT6	Capital Gains Tax – Retirement: Disposal of a business
IR74	Deeds of Covenant – getting it right for tax	CGT13	The Indexation Allowance for Quoted Shares
IR77	Taxation of Maintenance Payments	CGT14	Capital Gains Tax
IR78	Personal Pensions	CGT15	A Guide for Married Couples
IR80	Income Tax and Married Couples	IHT3	Inheritance Tax
IR82	Independent Taxation – A Guide for Husbands on a Low Income		

*available from your local tax office. See "Inland Revenue" in telephone directory.

CHAPTER 5

Tax Treatment of Your Investments

With few exceptions, most forms of interest are taxable and must be declared on your tax return, even if 20 per cent rate tax has been deducted at source.

If you haven't been sent a tax return and have untaxed interest to declare, it is still your legal responsibility to declare it; ring up your tax office for a tax return.

For basic rate and lower rate taxpayers, interest on savings and dividend income is subject to tax at a 20 per cent savings rate. If it is deducted at source, higher rate taxpayers must pay the difference between the 20 per cent savings rate and their own 40 per cent tax rate.

Tax-free investments

Tax-free investments do not have to be declared on the tax return. Tax-free income includes interest on conventional and index-linked National Savings Certificates, National Savings Yearly Plan, SAYE and Premium Bond winnings. Interest on Tax Exempt Special Savings Accounts will be tax free if reinvested; if the income is withdrawn it will be paid net, but the tax withheld is paid as tax-free bonus after five years if the capital is not withdrawn before.

Tax-free income which does not have to be declared on your tax return are the dividends paid on investments in a Personal Equity Plan. There is no capital gains tax payable on the proceeds. Husband and wife can each take out one Personal Equity Plan each tax year.

Tax-free income which does have to be declared on your tax return is the first £70 of interest from a National Savings Bank Ordinary Account or £140 in the case of a joint account. Husband and wife can each earn up to £70 a year tax free from their individual Ordinary Accounts.

The interest is declared on your tax return, because any excess over £70 which you might have earned from that account is taxable.

Bank, Building Society, Deposit Taker and Local Authority loan and interest

Since 6 April 1996 banks, building societies, deposit takers and local authorities (in respect of their fixed term loans), all pay interest either without deduction of tax for those registered as non-taxpayers or with 20 per cent rate tax deducted at source.

It means that lower rate and basic rate taxpayers have no further tax liability in respect of their investment, although it must still be declared on the tax return. However, higher rate taxpayers must pay

TAX TREATMENT OF YOUR INVESTMENTS

higher rate taxes on the interest. Non-taxpayers who fail to register (forms are provided in bank and building society branches) will be able to reclaim the tax paid on their interest.

In respect of joint accounts where one partner pays tax and the other is a non-taxpayer, most building societies and some banks will pay half the interest net and the other half gross.

Older taxpayers of modest income who might qualify for Age Allowance, the extra tax relief given to those over 65, and more still to those over 75, should be careful with interest which comes "tax paid". On the tax return it has to be declared gross – that is, as though tax had not been deducted at source – in order to calculate one's total income. This is often overlooked when calculating whether or not one is entitled to the age allowance. Tax-free National Savings, such as Certificates, or Personal Equity Plans are a good investment for borderline incomes.

To gross up "tax paid" interest

Divide the tax paid interest by 80 and multiply by 100, e.g.

i) Net interest of £80

$$\frac{80}{80} \times 100 = £100 \text{ gross interest}$$

ii) Net interest of £100

$$\frac{100}{80} \times 100 = £125 \text{ gross interest}$$

Higher rate taxpayers must also gross up the tax paid interest to work out their extra tax liability, e.g.

i) Net interest of £85 = £100 gross

A 40% rate taxpayer must pay 20% tax (i.e. 40% – 20%, the savings rate already paid) on that interest = £20 extra tax to be paid.

Net interest of £80 – £20 higher rate tax = interest net of 40% = £60.

ii) Net interest of £100 = £125 gross.

A 40% rate taxpayer must pay 20% more tax (i.e. 40% – 20%, the savings rate already paid) on that interest = £25 extra tax to be paid.

Net interest of £100 – £25 higher rate tax = interest net of 40% = £75.

Inland Revenue check

Although the interest from all these forms of investment is tax paid (unless the saver is registered as a non-taxpayer), the institutions are obliged to notify the Inland Revenue where interest has been paid.

From 6 April 1992 all interest paid has to be notified to the Inland Revenue.

National Savings Accounts, Government Stock (held on the National Savings Stock Register) and Offshore Investments which pay interest gross

The two National Savings Bank accounts (the Ordinary and Investment), National Savings Income Bonds and Pensioners Guaranteed Income Bonds, Government Stock bought from the National Savings Stock Register, War Loan, and interest from abroad is paid without deduction of tax – and these are therefore particularly appropriate forms of investment for non-taxpayers.

For taxpayers there are special rules for working out the tax on their gross interest, which depends on when they were bought. The tax is payable on 1 January of the year of assessment.

i) In the first tax year in which they are bought (tax years run from 6 April to the following 5 April), you are taxed on the actual interest you receive or have credited to you in that tax year. You declare the interest on your tax return for that year and will receive an assessment a few months later and be expected to pay the tax due within 30 days.

ii) In the second tax year, the same applies.

iii) In the third tax year, you are taxed on the interest you received in the *previous* year; or you can choose to pay tax on the interest you actually receive in that tax year (a worthwhile option if the interest is lower.

iv) In the fourth and subsequent years you pay tax on the interest you received in the previous year.

v) When you close an account, in that tax year you are charged tax on the actual interest you receive in that tax year.

vi) In the penultimate tax year, you normally pay tax on the previous year's interest (see iv above), but if you have by then closed the account, your tax assessment might be revised so that you pay tax on the actual interest received that year if it is higher.

If the amount of tax due is relatively small, the Inland Revenue might collect it by adjusting your PAYE tax code number downwards, instead of asking for a lump sum payment.

Shares and unit trusts

Dividend income from shares and unit trusts is paid net of 20 per cent rate tax. Non-taxpayers can reclaim the tax paid, while higher rate taxpayers will have to pay the difference between basic and higher rates.

Dividend income from shares has tax deducted at source in the form of a "tax credit" which is 20 per cent.

Higher rate taxpayers pay the difference between 20 per cent and the higher rate of tax of 40 per cent on their dividend income. Investors who are non-taxpayers or low taxpayers will only be able to reclaim 20 per cent.

The same situation applies to the distribution paid by unit trusts to their unitholders.

Life insurance policies

Although life insurance companies pay tax, which affects the position of their life funds (in which your money is placed), most life insurance policy proceeds – the sum you collect at maturity or death – are free of both income and capital gains tax. The capital gains tax that life offices have to pay on their life funds is reflected in the underlying value of the investments; or with some unit-linked policies, a deduction for capital gains tax might be made from the proceeds of a policy you encash.

With investment bonds or single premium insurance bonds, higher rate taxpayers may be liable to higher rate tax *only* on the proceeds; or on the proceeds of a regular premium policy encashed before three-quarters of the original term has been reached or within 10 years (whichever is less).

At the moment up to 5 per cent of the original investment can be withdrawn as "income" from investment bonds with the tax liability deferred until the bond is encashed or within 20 years, if earlier. However, plans to reform the taxation of life policies are likely to result in this facility being withdrawn in future.

The objective for higher rate taxpayers is to defer the tax liability until a date when their tax will be lower. For both higher rate taxpayers and older taxpayers who are on the age allowance borderline, the attraction of such a plan is that the "income" does not have to be declared on the tax return.

When higher rate taxpayers encash their investment bonds, "top slicing relief" is applied to reduce the tax liability by taking into account the number of years the investment has been held. Average the profit over the number of years the bond has been in place; add the amount to the policyholder's income to arrive at the higher rate tax owing.

Policyholders who took out regular premium policies before 13 March 1984 are still eligible for life assurance tax relief of 12½ per cent on the premiums. The relief is deducted from the premiums so that only the net amount is payable. Hang on to such policies, unless there are compelling reasons to stop paying.

TAX TREATMENT OF YOUR INVESTMENTS

Personal pensions

The self-employed and those not in an occupational pension scheme have for a long time been able to build up a pension entitlement for themselves with a self-employed retirement annuity, often known as Section 226 policies. These have been replaced by personal pension plans which are available to both the self-employed and employees who do not have a company pension scheme to join, or elect not to join or remain in a company pension scheme.

Tax relief, at your highest rate, is given on personal pension plan contributions up to an earnings limit currently of £84,000 for entrants from 6 April 1989 onwards at the following rates:

Up to age 35	17½%
Up to age 36–45	20%
Up to age 46–50	25%
Up to age 51–55	30%
Up to age 56–60	35%
61 and over	40%

In addition, employees can come out of the SERPS (State Earnings Related Pension Scheme), and the Government will invest into your personal pension plan the relevant National Insurance "contracting out" rebates for both employer and employee totalling 4.8 per cent, plus a 1 per cent age-related rebate for those over 30. New age-related rebate terms (for all age groups) are expected later in 1996.

Investment is made in a tax-free investment fund, managed by a life insurance company. Other institutions such as building societies are providing personal pension plans too.

Pension investment is long term. Except for certain jobs with early "retirement" such as divers or professional sportsmen, Section 226 pensions cannot be taken, at the moment, until age 60; with personal pension plans retirement age can be as low as 50, but few people will have earned enough to take their pension so young. The latest you can retire is 75.

When you retire you can either take an annuity (income for life) from the company running your pensions policy or shop around and buy your annuity from another company if it offers better rates.

Since 1996 it has been possible to defer taking your annuity for up to five years. This is useful if your retirement happens to come at a time when annuity rates are low.

Although the pension will be taxable, part of the proceeds of a personal pension plan can be taken as a lump sum, but for policies taken out after 17 March 1987, that is limited to £150,000.

Late starters who have delayed their pension planning can carry back up to six years of pension plan contributions.

Provided you have set aside the maximum amount of contribution for the current year, you can then top up the preceding tax years' contributions for a total of six years, starting with the earliest relevant year. Tax relief is given at current tax rates.

With Section 226 policies the contribution ceilings are different. There is no earnings cap.

Up to age 50	17½%
Up to age 51–55	20%
Up to age 56–60	22½%
Up to age 61–75	27½%

For the relevant tax years 1982–83 to 1986–87 the contribution rates were based on the year in which you were born.

after 1933	17½%
1916–1933	20%
1914–1915	21%
1912–1913	24%
1910–1911	26½%
1908–1909	29½%
1907 or earlier	32½%

No tax relief is given on contributions made after age 75 years.

CHAPTER 6

Savings and the Family

There has been a revolution in how families are taxed which has significant implications for the way we save money. Since 6 April 1990, a husband and wife have been treated as separate individuals, each with their own personal allowance. And irrespective of whether a wife's income is earned or unearned she is still able to set it against her personal allowance. (Previously, a wife's unearned income was always, from a tax point of view, treated as belonging to her husband.)

It means that from now on, each partner in the marriage is able to enjoy tax-free income of £4,045 (the level of the new personal allowance). In addition, there is the married couple's allowance of £1,830 which, in the first instance, will go to the husband but which can be transferred to the wife if his income is insufficient.

Since 6 April 1995 tax relief on the married couple's allowance has been given at the 15 per cent tax rate only irrespective of the spouses' tax brackets.

In addition, each spouse is now entitled to their own capital gains tax exemption of the first £6,500 of gains in the year.

In order to maximise the family's income, it therefore makes sense to make full use of the wife's personal allowance – even if she is not working. The simplest way is to increase her savings so that she has investment income to offset against her allowance. Tax-free investments, which have hitherto been the most sensible form of investment for her, no longer fit the bill. She needs income which is either paid gross (that is before tax) or net, but on which she can reclaim any basic rate tax paid on her behalf.

For example why should she bother with a Tax Exempt Special Savings Account? She can obtain gross interest without tying up capital for five years, and she will not be able to offset the interest against her personal allowance. Similarly the tax-free income from a Personal Equity Plan will not help reduce her personal allowance.

With gross interest rates of 6–8 per cent, she can have savings of around £45,000 – and not pay tax on the interest. However, it must be from her money. If a husband gives his wife capital to invest in this tax efficient way, and the marriage subsequently fails, he cannot demand the money back. It will be hers.

Where a couple have savings in a joint name, the taxman will deem that half the interest belongs to the wife and half to the husband. If you don't want to split the income from a joint holding on a 50–50 basis, you must let the Inland Revenue know how you want it apportioned.

Investments for Non-Working Wives
  Building Society Accounts
  National Savings Investment Account
  National Savings Income Bonds

High Yielding Unit Trusts
High Yielding Investment Trusts

Investments Not Suitable for a Non-Working Wife
National Savings Certificates
Personal Equity Plans
Tax Exempt Special Savings Account

Children

All children are potential taxpayers and entitled to the single person's tax allowance in respect of any interest they earn, with one important exception. As they are unlikely to be taxpayers, parents should register them as non-taxpayers to receive bank or building society interest gross. Grandparents cannot do this on behalf of their grandchildren.

Income from any money given by parent(s) is, apart from the first £100, treated as the donor parent's for tax purposes. State child benefit, saved for a child, counts as a gift of money from the parent.

The one exception to the rule is when money is given to the child "absolutely" in trust, and the income accumulated until the child is 18 or marries.

So children's savings fall into two categories with the following provisos:

The interest earned on gifts of money from a parent to child is tax free provided it does not exceed £100. If the interest is over £100 then the *entire* interest is counted as the parent's and taxed at his or her top rate of income tax. Each parent can make separate gifts where the interest does not exceed £100. This rate only applies to parental gifts: gifts from grandparents, etc, are not caught.

Interest on tax-free investments are sometimes so low that they compare unfavourably with net (after tax) returns elsewhere. Parents must decide which is more important: a lower tax bill for themselves, or a better return for their children. In such circumstances, the gift could come via a non-working mother who still has some of her own personal tax allowance to use up.

a) Savings from parental gifts
This includes pocket money and child benefit invested on the child's behalf. The money should be in savings where the interest is tax free.

Building Society Children's Account
Bank Children's Account
Building Society Instant Access Account
National Savings Certificates
National Savings Children's Bonus Bond

b) Savings from all other sources
This includes birthday gifts, savings from Saturday jobs and other cash windfalls. For greatest convenience, the money should be in savings where the interest is paid gross (see above).

National Savings Bank Investment Account
National Savings Children's Bonus Bonds
Government Stock on the National Savings Stock Register
Offshore bank accounts

Alternatively, children's money can be in investments, such as shares and unit trusts, where basic rate tax is deducted at source but can be reclaimed by non-taxpayers. Use Tax Claim Form R40 to reclaim tax on behalf of a child.

Children need to learn about money management. Sometimes the investment for long-term savings which pays the most interest and has the most efficient tax structure, such as the National Savings Bank Investment Account (it requires one month's notice to withdraw funds) or the Children's Bonus Bond, might not be the most suitable for the week-to-week money transactions.

CHAPTER 7

The Essential Savings

In Chapter One, we identified the four types of essential savings which all families should consider; single persons might be able to opt out of one of them – financial protection for dependants.

Emergency savings

You may get no advance warning when a financial emergency strikes, so you must have money easily available to meet those unexpected bills and out-of-the-blue demands on your pocket.

The only question is how large your emergency fund should be. To a certain extent this depends on your family circumstances. A family with a chronically sick child, for example, will almost certainly need a larger emergency fund; and the self-employed will fear the cash consequences of sickness more. If you are well placed to borrow money to meet emergencies, then you might prefer to have less in your immediate emergency fund.

Between £500 and £3,000 is a suitable amount for an emergency fund. As a rule of thumb, up to three months' pay is the amount a family should consider for its emergency fund. Higher earners can probably think in terms of less; young single persons, too, will probably reduce that target. For people of modest resources, an emergency fund might be their only form of saving. If you haven't got a lump sum to earmark for emergencies, set about building one up with regular savings which carry no penalties if you have to stop saving to draw on the fund.

Because it is a fund designed for emergencies, these savings must be accessible on demand and in full. This restricts the choice to a range of bank, building society, deposit taker and offshore accounts.

In addition, the physical convenience and networks of these institutions have to be taken into account. If your emergency fund is set at quite a high level, you need not have all of it at immediate notice. Seven-day notice periods and even as long as a month's notice can be acceptable for the second tier of your emergency savings.

Do not forget that once your emergency fund has been tapped, it will either need replacing or topping up to the desired level. Bring back your second level of emergency savings to immediate access accounts, and then replace that level of savings from other sources.

Lump sum savings immediately available

Bank Deposit Account (small penalty)
Bank High Interest Cheque Account
Bank Savings Accounts

Building Society Instant Access (provided minimum balance maintained)
Building Society Ordinary Account
Offshore High Interest Cheque Account
Offshore Single Currency Fund
National Savings Ordinary Account

Lump sum savings available within a month

Bank High Interest Deposit Account
Bank Notice Account (some)
Building Society Notice Account (some)
National Savings Bank Investment Account
National Savings Certificates (small penalty)
National Savings Index-Linked Certificates
National Savings Premium Bond

Regular Savings

Building Society Monthly Savings Account

A Tax Exempt Special Savings Account (Tessa) is suitable for regular savings. Designed to be held for five years, the capital can be withdrawn earlier but you will have to sacrifice the tax-free bonus on the interest earned. If you have to dip into your Tessa for an emergency, then it becomes just like another building society account. If you are fortunate and emergencies don't strike, then your Tessa retains its tax-free benefits.

Financial protection for your family

If you die prematurely, your wife and children will need capital and/or income to replace your earnings. If you are unable to work through ill-health or disability they will need capital and/or income to replace your savings.

Most of your savings and investments will form part of your estate and be tied up until probate (if you have made a will) or letters of administration (if you have not) has been granted.

Even more to the point, are your savings and investments sufficient to provide adequate financial protection for your dependants?

Life insurance policies, written in trust for the benefit of a man's wife (or wife's husband) and/or his (her) children, will, on the death of the policy-holder, immediately pay out the proceeds (the sum assured plus any bonuses which might have been added) without waiting for either a grant of probate or letters of administration.

The sum assured is likely to be considerably larger than your savings, particularly if you are a younger person. One guideline is that your life insurance cover should be up to five times salary, including your endowment mortgage, mortgage protection policy and any death-in-service pension scheme benefits.

Permanent health insurance policies will pay an income for the rest of your working life should you be unable to work.

Critical illness cover is now widely available. It pays out if you are struck by a serious illness such as cancer, kidney failure or heart condition.

The life insurance contracts discussed in the second section of the book are basically to be considered as investments, as their life insurance element is minimal.

Saving for a house

Although it is sometimes possible to obtain a 100 per cent home loan, most people, wisely, prefer to save for a home. If mortgage funds are in short supply, regular savings will also help secure your mortgage.

Consider:
   Bank Monthly Savings Account
   Mortgage Savings Account
   Building Society Monthly Savings Account

Lump sum savings towards your own home should not be locked away for longer than one to three months.

Consider:
> Building Society Instant Access Account
> Building Society Notice Account
> Bank High Interest Deposit Account
> National Savings Bank Investment Account

Saving for retirement

Apart from the basic state pension, paid for from National Insurance contributions, everyone should now be entitled to a second pension through a company pension scheme, personal pension plan or state earnings related scheme (SERPS).

The question is whether your pension will be large enough in retirement. Many people began making their pension arrangements later in life and might not have made sufficient pension payments to look forward to a financially comfortable retirement.

With the help of your pension scheme manager, check the current day value of your future pension, and compare it with your current expenditure. If the shortfall between the two is too large today, it will almost certainly be too large when you reach retirement.

Employees can augment their retirement pension by:

Additional Voluntary Contributions – either to the company pension scheme, or to a "free-standing" AVC scheme of your own choice.

The **self-employed** can augment their retirement pension by:

Further contribution to a Self-Employed Retirement Annuity (taken out before 1 July 1988), or the Personal Pension Plan which succeeded it. Then carry forward contributions to top up premiums for earlier tax years.

If you want to save more than the maximum annual savings (expressed as a percentage of income) permitted to these schemes or don't wish to commit your savings irrevocably towards pensions, then consider:

> Life Insurance – With-Profits Endowment Policy
> Life Insurance – With-Profits Flexible Endowment Policy
> Life Insurance – Unit-Linked Savings Plan
> Shares – Personal Equity Plans
> Shares – Unit Trust and Investment Trust Savings Plans

For lump sum investments to build up your future capital for retirement, consider:

> Life Insurance – Investment Bonds
> Offshore – Managed Currency Fund
> Shares – Investment Trust and Unit Trust
> Shares – Ordinary
> Shares – Personal Equity Plans

CHAPTER 8

Savings Strategies

Short-term savings

Holidays, cars and weddings are three important reasons why people save; and most people have a fairly clear idea of how much they wish to spend on each.

For holidays, *consider:*
    Bank High Interest Deposit Account
    Bank High Interest Cheque Account
    Building Society Instant Access Account
    National Savings Bank Investment Account
    Offshore High Interest Cheque Account
    Offshore Single Currency Fund – for spending money

For cars, *consider:*
    Building Society Monthly Savings Account
    Building Society Instant Access Account
    National Savings Bank Investment Account

For weddings, *consider:*
    Holidays list if the wedding is within the coming 12 months
    Cars list, if the wedding is longer than 12 months away

There are inheritance tax exemptions for family gifts of money to the bride and groom (see Chapter Four).

School fees

If you plan to educate your child privately, the earlier you start saving towards your offspring's future school fees, the better. The Assisted Places Scheme cuts the burden of school fees for less well-off parents. (Phone Independent Schools Information Service – 0171–630 8793 – for more details.)

For regular savings towards future school fees needed in five or more years, consider:
    Bank or Building Society
    Tax Exempt Special Savings Account
    Shares – Personal Equity Plans

For savings towards school fees needed in 10 or more years, consider:
    Bank or Building Society
    Tax Exempt Special Savings Account
    Shares – Personal Equity Plans
    Shares – Unit Trust Monthly Savings Schemes
    Shares – Investment Trust Monthly Savings Scheme
    Life Insurance – With-Profits Flexible Policy

For lump sums for school fees, consider:
    Life Insurance – Growth Bond
    Life Insurance – Investment Bond
    Life Insurance – School Fees Educational Trust
    Shares – Unit Trusts, Investment Trusts

Stock – Government Fixed Interest, Government Index-Linked

An accumulation and maintenance trust is suitable for larger lump sums donated for the purposes of school fees by someone other than the parent, such as grandparent or godparent. There are tax advantages (see Chapter Three). A solicitor or accountant will advise you on setting up a trust.

Divorce

Maintenance payments under a court order or enforceable separation deed made after 14 March 1988 are tax free in the hands of the recipient. Under agreements made before then, payments to a spouse above £1,830 count as taxable income; payments to a child are taxable, but the child has the single person's allowance of £4,045 to offset against it.

The payer will not be entitled to tax relief on payments made under post 14 March 1988 agreements, except up to a limit equal to the difference between the personal allowance and married couple's allowance, now £1,830. The relief will only apply at the lower, 15 per cent tax band.

If a cash settlement is made, suitable investments to provide a regular income are:

Building Society Monthly Income Account
National Savings Income Bond
Shares – Unit Trust Monthly Income Scheme

Divorce invalidates wills, widow's or widower's pension rights (unless a judge orders otherwise) and affects life insurance policies where the proceeds are in trust for a wife/husband. Both parties should check their position.

Redundancy

Only the first £30,000 of a lump sum redundancy payment is tax free.

If you are over 50, you might be given retirement as well as redundancy and be entitled to a pension and cash commutation of your pension rights; this lump sum is also tax free.

Unemployment benefit, which lasts for up to one year, is taxable. If you are still unemployed, then you might qualify for income support, which is tax free, provided your savings do not exceed £3,000.

Whether you are planning to go into business on your own, or feel you might have to delve into your redundancy money for survival, the same rule applies: do not tie up your money for anything longer than one to three months, and be sure that you can get your money back in full. If you consider your unemployment as early retirement, look at the later sections in this chapter on retirement.

Lump sum investments

Bank High Interest Cheque Account
Bank High Interest Deposit Account
Building Society Instant Access Account
Building Society Notice Account
National Savings Bank Investment Account
Offshore High Interest Cheque Account

Widowhood

Widows get the widow's bereavement tax allowance of £1,830 both in the tax year of the husband's death and the following tax year too. A widow with children will also get the additional personal allowance for children. Both of these allowances can only be set against the 15 per cent tax band.

Widow's pensions and widowed mother's allowances are taxable; the child addition paid to the widow's benefit, if applicable, is tax free.

Any life insurance payable on her husband's death is tax free, even if it is paid in regular instalments as a family income benefit. A widow's pension from her husband's company pension scheme is taxable.

Some widows inherit substantial investment portfolios, and should take professional advice about them if they are inexperienced investors.

IFA Promotion Helpline 0117–971 1177 will

supply a list of three independent financial advisers in your locality.

Non-working widows who are wanting monthly income should consider:

Building Society Monthly Income Account
National Savings Income Bond
National Savings Pensioners Guaranteed Income Bond (if over 60 years old)

and for future growth:

Shares – Unit Trust Monthly Income Plan

Retirement

The extra tax allowance for those over 65 and on modest incomes needs careful planning.

Anyone over 65 is entitled to the personal age allowance of £5,220. The married couple's allowance of £3,185 goes initially to the husband. If he is under 65 and his wife over 65, special arrangements are made.

When your income exceeds £15,600, the extra age allowance is reduced by £1 for every £2 of income until it is finally extinguished and you are on the normal tax allowance level. For the individual, this occurs when income reaches £17,950, for the person claiming the married couple's allowance it is £20,660.

There is an extra age allowance of £5,400 (personal) and £3,225 (married) for those over 75. The income limit remains £15,600; therefore the extra age allowance is reduced by £1 for every £2 of income until it is extinguished at £18,310 (personal), £21,100 (including married couple's allowance).

It is important to keep your income under the threshold of £15,600 if you are a borderline case, and look for income which does not have to be declared on your tax return.

Consider:

Bank or Building Society – Tax Exempt Special Savings Account

Life Assurance – Investment Bond 5 per cent withdrawal plan
National Savings Certificates – cashing units each year to provide an "income" and leaving your capital intact
Shares – Personal Equity Plan

Do not forget to gross up the interest paid by banks, building societies, deposit takers and local authorities in calculating your total income. If your total income is near the £15,600 level, the gross interest could result in some lost personal allowance. See Chapter Five.

Retirement can last a long time, and although more and more company pensions are increasing payments, it is not wise (if you have sufficient capital for a spread of investment) to have the rest of your retirement savings entirely in fixed capital investments. Interest rates can go down.

Consider:

Bank and Building Society – Tax Exempt Special Savings Account
Building Society Instant Access
Bank High Interest Cheque Account
Offshore High Interest Account
National Savings Income Bonds
National Savings Pensioners Guaranteed Income Bond (if over 60 years old)
Shares – Unit Trust – Monthly Income Plan
Shares – Investment Trusts

Very old

Annuities begin to look attractive for men and women in their seventies. Home income plans, a way of boosting retirement income by using the capital tied up in your own home, are available to individuals over 70 and married couples with a joint age of 150 years.

CHAPTER 9

Investor Protection

There are two kinds of risk facing the investor.

Investment risk is the possibility of losing some, even all, of your money in an asset which fluctuates in value (see Chapter Two).

The other kind of risk investors take is that the body or institution looking after their money might go bust; or that the person or organisation handling your investments might go bust or fail to invest your money for you.

Various safeguards exist to protect investors from such eventualities, however unlikely they might be in some cases. And if the worst were to happen, compensation schemes will provide some financial consolation.

Financial Services Act

This major piece of investor protection legislation came into force in 1988. It created the Securities and Investments Board (SIB) to vet and authorise all investment businesses. Until 1994 this was done through a variety of watch-dog organisations covering different aspects of the financial services industry.

Following a major overhaul of the system, the Personal Investment Authority (PIA) was set up in July 1994 to oversee and regulate all the investment organisations which do business with private investors.

The companies and organisations which are now vetted and monitored by the PIA are life insurance companies and unit trust activities (previously controlled by LAUTRO), independent financial advisers (previously under the wing of FIMBRA), friendly societies and also banks and building societies in respect of their growing life assurance business.

All companies with retail investment business must have registered with the PIA. It is a criminal offence to carry on an investment business without being authorised by the PIA.

There may be one or two exceptions which are registered directly with SIB.

The PIA Helpline number deals with all initial enquiries including calls regarding LAUTRO and FIMBRA (tel: 0171–538 8860).

SIB continues to hold a complete list of all authorised firms or individuals. Make sure that your investment adviser, fund manager or stockbroker is authorised by calling 0171–929 3652. You will be told the firm's full name, head office address and the areas of business the firm is authorised to deal in.

If something goes wrong with your investment or savings there are two kinds of safeguards:
* statutory compensation schemes to protect you if the company handling your money fails and your money is lost;
* ombudsmen who can investigate complaints of maladministration, negligence or unfairness. If an

ombudsman decides in favour of the individual saver or policyholder, he can order the offending company to make financial restitution.

Compensation Schemes

The **SIB Compensation Scheme** covers 100 per cent of the first £30,000 of savings and 90 per cent of the next £20,000 making an overall maximum compensation of £48,000.

The **Bank Deposit Protection** scheme provides compensation of 90 per cent of the £20,000 of deposits.

The **Building Societies Compensation** scheme provides compensation of 90 per cent of savings up to £20,000, a maximum of £18,000 no matter how many accounts a saver has with that society.

The **Policyholders Protection Act** provides 90 per cent of policy benefits, provided these are not 'excessive'.

The **Government** guarantees National Savings.

Ombudsmen Schemes

The **PIA Ombudsman** will investigate complaints and grievances against members of the PIA. In respect of life assurance complaints he has effectively taken over from the Insurance Ombudsman. Awards of up to £50,000 against an offending company are binding, and he can recommend awards up to £100,000 (tel: 0171–538 8860).

The **Building Societies Ombudsman** will investigate intractable complaints which have not been resolved by a society's own complaints procedure. The maximum award is £100,000 and is binding on societies (tel: 0171–931 0044).

The **Banking Ombudsman** will investigate complaints which have not been resolved by a bank's own complaints procedure. The maximum award is £100,000 and is binding on banks (tel: 0171–404 9944).

The **Insurance Ombudsman**'s role has been scaled to largely dealing with complaints about general insurance (tel: 0171–928 4488).

The **Pensions Ombudsman** investigates complaints about company pension schemes. In the first place, complaints must go to OPAS, the Occupational Pensions Advisory Service to assess whether the grievance should go to the Ombudsman (tel: 0171–233 8080).

The **PIA Pensions Unit** has been set up to assist people who are worried that they have been mis-sold a personal pension plan since 1988 (tel: 0171–417 7001).

Others

The PIA has not taken over the duties of the SFA and IMRO which still referee stockbrokers and fund managers. Each has a compensation scheme which mirrors SIBs and there is an IMRO referee who deals with complaints.

IMRO – the Investment Managers Regulatory Organisation covers all investment management organisations such as unit trust groups, pension fund and life insurance fund management (tel: 0171–390 5000).

SFA – the Securities & Futures Authority covers stockbrokers and securities dealers and includes the former Association of Futures Brokers and Dealers (tel: 0171–378 9000). If the SFA's own Complaints Bureau cannot reconcile the dispute, you can take your claim (up to £50,000) to an independent arbitration scheme. The arbitrator's award is final and binding.

CHAPTER 10

High Street Banks (and Others*)

Children's Account

Children's bank accounts may offer a range of free gifts and magazines. Some banks now have a separate account for older children and young people with a cash dispenser card. Midland, TSB and Yorkshire are the most active banks on the school banking scene.

Suitable for	Children's pocket money and encouraging money management.
Open to	Children up to 16, occasionally 14. Thereafter account reverts to instant access account.
Min–Max	Ranges from £1–£10; no maximum.
Withdrawals	Either seven days' notice (or loss of seven days' interest if immediate) or immediate withdrawal. Instant cash dispenser withdrawals allowed in most cases for young people over 13 years.
Interest	Variable; usually paid half-yearly into account. Banks can pay interest gross to non-taxpayers.
Children	Yes, but parent's signature is required for withdrawals for under-sevens.

* includes telephone banks, UK subsidiaries of foreign banks and finance houses. All are "authorised institutions" under The Banking Act 1987.

HIGH STREET BANKS (AND OTHERS)

How to invest	Apply at a bank branch. Obtain form to register child as non-taxpayer from branch. Only parents can sign on behalf of a child.
Record	Half-yearly statements and paying-in books.
Money Mail Rating	*****
Investor protection	Bank savings compensation scheme covers 90 per cent of savings up to £20,000. Maximum payout £18,000 per person.
Comment	Convenience, including a Saturday morning branch (as banking hours do not fit in with school hours), and highest available interest rate should be just as important as the free gifts, money boxes and magazines! Check whether your local building society children's schemes offer a higher rate of interest; the gifts will be less impressive. For larger sums, consider money which can be "locked up", possibly with a higher interest rate.

Deposit Account

Old-style bank interest-bearing account requiring seven days' notice to withdraw funds or loss of seven days' interest if withdrawn immediately. No cheque book.

Suitable for	Lump sums below the threshold for Instant Access or Notice Accounts, but not recommended.
Open to	Anyone.
Min–Max	£1 minimum; no maximum.
Withdrawals	Any amount at seven days' notice, or immediately with loss of seven days' interest.

Interest	Variable, usually paid half-yearly either to this account or current account.
Tax	Interest is paid net of 20 per cent tax; higher rate taxpayers pay difference of 20 per cent tax more. Banks can pay interest gross to non-taxpayers.
Children	Yes, but Bank Children's Account a better investment.
How to invest	At any branch of most banks. You need not have a current account with the bank. Register at branch to obtain gross interest if non-taxpayer.
Record	Usually none. Half-yearly statement. Keep paying-in slip stubs.
Money Mail Rating	*****
Investor protection	Bank savings compensation scheme covers 90 per cent of savings up to £20,000.
Comment	It is hard to make a case for continuing in a Bank Deposit Account which pays the lowest rate of interest of all bank accounts, and less than building society ordinary account. Non-taxpayers should consider a National Savings Investment Account.

High Interest Cheque Account

Interest-bearing current account, usually with minimum starting investment, often £2,000–£2,500. It is a cheque-book account, but some banks stipulate minimum cheque withdrawal of £200–£250. Standing orders and overdrafts are allowed; sometimes run primarily in conjunction with group's investment management arm. Debit card facility usually included, occasionally a credit card as well. Cheque guarantee facility usually £100.

Suitable for	Investors with frequent high value transactions such as school fees and large household bills; bank customers who habitually keep too much in their current account or keep household running funds in an interest-bearing but less flexible building society account.

HIGH STREET BANKS (AND OTHERS)

Open to — Anyone aged 18 or over.

Min–Max — Minimum commonly £2,000–£2,500, but can be as low as £500. No maximum.

Charges — Usually free banking if in credit; limited number of free cheques at some banks.

Withdrawals — Sometimes minimum cheque withdrawal of £200–£250, but most groups have no minimum cheque withdrawals. Where a credit card is part of the package, monthly repayment can be below minimum cheque level.

Interest — Variable, calculated daily; sometimes a tiered rate so larger amounts earn more. Make sure you keep the minimum opening balance in the account or you will get a very low interest rate.

Tax — Interest is paid net of 20 per cent tax; higher rate taxpayers pay difference of 20 per cent tax more. Banks can pay interest gross to non-taxpayers; non-taxpayers who fail to register as such will still be able to reclaim the basic rate tax deducted at source.

Children — Not unless account held in adult's name.

How to invest — Apply in writing or through branch network to Abbey National, Allied Trust Bank, Bank of Ireland, Bank of Scotland, Barclays, Caledonian Bank, Cater Allen, Clydesdale, Kleinwort Benson, Lloyds, Midland, National Westminster, Royal Bank of Scotland, Save & Prosper (Robert Fleming), Schroder, Tyndall, Western Trust.

Record — Bank statement, usually quarterly.

Money Mail Rating — *****

Investor protection — Bank savings compensation scheme covers 90 per cent of savings up to £20,000. Maximum payout £18,000 per person.

37

Comment	With full banking facilities – cheque guarantee card, standing order payments and overdrafts – this account can replace the current account entirely, provided you can meet the conditions such as limited cheque withdrawals or high value withdrawals only. It is not a savings account.

Instant Access Account

This is the banks' answer to the key building society instant access account. An easy access high interest account, with a minimum balance of often at least £1,000, frequently with a tiered interest rate structure so that larger amounts earn more. A monthly income facility is sometimes included. A cash card is available as part of the package.

Suitable for	Lump sum investments for emergencies, day-to-day money management, irregular savings, "rainy day" money.
Open to	Anyone.
Min–Max	As little as £1 but £500–£2,000 is more common minimum; no maximum.
Charges	None.
Withdrawals	On demand from any branch.
Interest	Variable, usually tiered so that larger sums earn more, paid quarterly or annually. Rates are usually higher than a High Interest Cheque Account.
Tax	Interest is paid net of 20 per cent tax; higher rate taxpayers pay difference of 20 per cent more. Banks can pay interest gross to non-taxpayers; non-taxpayers who fail to fill in the self-certification form will still be able to reclaim the basic rate tax deducted at source.
Children	Yes, but parent's signature for withdrawals for under-sevens.

HIGH STREET BANKS (AND OTHERS)

How to invest	At branch or apply in writing to Abbey National, Allied Trust, Barclays, Clydesdale, Co-operative Bank, First Direct, Girobank, Lloyds, Midland, National Westminster, Royal Bank of Scotland, TSB, Tyndall.
Record	Bank statement.
Money Mail Rating	*****
Investor protection	Bank savings compensation scheme covers 90 per cent of savings up to £20,000. Maximum payout £18,000 per person.
Comment	Always compare rates with building society instant access accounts. Make sure you do not get stuck in an obsolete account – newer versions usually pay more, but don't expect to be told to switch!

Interest-Bearing Current Account

In the wake of increased competition from building societies, most of the High Street banks have launched one or more current accounts which pay interest. Such an account should not be viewed as an investment. More and more banks are offering 24 hour telephone banking facilities to this account.

Suitable for	Day-to-day money management for people who habitually keep their current accounts in credit.
Open to	Anyone over 18.
Min–Max	£1; no maximum.
Charges	Free if account in credit. Often a monthly or quarterly fee for overdrawn customers.
Withdrawals	On demand.

Interest	Variable, and often tiered so that large balances earn more.
Tax	Interest is paid net of 20 per cent tax; higher rate taxpayers will pay difference between 20 per cent tax more. Banks can pay interest gross to non-taxpayers; non-taxpayers who fail to register will still be able to reclaim the basic rate tax deducted at source.
Children	No, if automatic loan facilities are included in the account package. Children's savings accounts can be converted later.
How to invest	At any branch of most banks.
Record	Regular statements.
Money Mail Rating	*****
Investor protection	Bank compensation scheme covers 90 per cent of credit balances up to £20,000. Maximum payout £18,000 per person.
Comment	Rates vary, so choose a bank with the best rate for your likely balance. Charges can be high if overdrawn over a certain limit, usually £100–£250, so these accounts are more suitable for individuals who retain a credit balance each month rather than going into the red. It's basically a current account and you should not build up surplus cash in this account.

Monthly Income Account

Lump sum investment, which can usually be increased at any time, which pays higher rate interest monthly into the customer's current account. Withdrawal notice period varies from none to six months.

Suitable for	Those needing to boost monthly income who have a current or other account for day-to-day money management.

HIGH STREET BANKS (AND OTHERS)

Open to	Anyone.
Min–Max	£1,000–£2,500 minimum; occasionally £500; no maximum.
Charges	None.
Withdrawals	Withdrawals after notice period if any.
Interest	Variable, paid monthly. Rates are tiered so that the more you invest, the more you earn; rates are substantially better for those with £10,000 or more. Abbey National, Allied Trust and First Direct normally pay competitive rates.
Tax	Interest is paid net of 20 per cent tax; higher rate taxpayers pay difference of 20 per cent tax more. Banks can pay interest gross to non-taxpayers; non-taxpayers who fail to register will still be able to reclaim the basic rate tax deducted at source.
Children	Not suitable.
How to invest	At any branch of most banks.
Record	Regular statements.
Money Mail Rating	*****
Investor protection	Bank savings compensation scheme covers 90 per cent of savings up to £20,000. Maximum payout £18,000 per person.
Comment	Always compare rates with building society monthly income accounts and the National Savings Income Bond.

Notice Account

Lump sum investment which requires notice of one, two, three or six months to withdraw funds. Investors have the option of losing interest for relevant period and instant access on funds.

HIGH STREET BANKS (AND OTHERS)

Suitable for   Relatively short-term "parking" of money not immediately required nor considered as part of your emergency money.

Open to   Anyone.

Min–Max   £100–£500 minimum. £25,000–£50,000 maximum.

Charges   None.

Withdrawals   Partial or full withdrawals permitted after specified notice period, or you can accept loss of interest if you withdraw before then. If you keep a balance, usually of £10,000, instant withdrawal from the surplus is usually allowed without penalty. National Westminster allows £250 a month withdrawal without penalty. Lombard North Central one penalty free withdrawal pa of 10 per cent of balance. Royal Bank of Scotland Royal Reward, 2 per cent bonus if no withdrawals pa.

Interest   Variable, usually paid half-yearly or quarterly. It can be paid by cheque, or direct into a bank account, or reinvested.

Tax   Interest is paid net of 20 per cent tax; higher rate taxpayers pay difference of 20 per cent tax more. Banks can pay interest gross to non-taxpayers; non-taxpayers who fail to register will still be able to reclaim the basic rate tax deducted at source.

Children   Yes; parent's signature normally required for under-sevens.

How to invest   Check interest rates at a local branch.

Investor protection   Bank savings compensation scheme covers 90 per cent of savings up to £20,000. Maximum payout £18,000 per person.

Comment   In general bank savings rates have become much more competitive in recent years. Compare interest rates and the minimum investment required with building society instant access accounts. Abbey National offers good 90 days' notice account, TSB 60 days' notice, and Barclays and National Westminster one month's notice.

HIGH STREET BANKS (AND OTHERS)

Save As You Earn (SAYE)

2nd Issue

This was withdrawn in November 1994 Budget. But existing holders should keep. Regular monthly savings scheme for five years with an option to leave your investment for a further two years. Interest, which accumulates, is tax free and in addition there is a bonus equivalent to 14 months' payments, tax free, at the end of five years, or 28 months' tax-free payments if you leave the savings in for the next two years. A gap of six months' savings can be made up.

Charges None.

Withdrawals No partial withdrawals; repayment takes two to three weeks. Reduced interest rate penalties on early withdrawals: no interest in year one, years two to five interest of 6 per cent only (8 per cent if you die).

Interest Fixed. Including the bonus, the rate is equivalent to 8.3 per cent a year over five years; including the enlarged bonus, the rate over seven years is equivalent to 8.62 per cent a year. It accumulates and is paid out when the contract matures.

Tax Tax free.

Money Mail Rating *****

Investor protection Bank savings compensation scheme covers 90 per cent of savings up to £20,000.

Comment Keep up the savings for five years; early surrender rates are unattractive.

Save As You Earn (SAYE)
Series "F" Share Option Scheme

Regular monthly savings linked to a company share option scheme. Employees are offered the option to buy shares at a price fixed at the start of the five-year savings period which cannot be less than 80 per cent of their market value. Employees invest a set amount each month in the SAYE scheme. At the end of five years they can either use the money to exercise the share option or take the money with a bonus. They can leave the money invested for another two years to obtain a higher bonus BUT they will then lose the share option entitlement. However, some employers offer a seven-year share option plan when the share option can then be exercised.

Interest in the SAYE accumulates tax free. In addition there is a bonus of 9 months' payments tax free at the end of five years, or 18 months' if you leave the savings in for the next two years.

Suitable for	Employees who want to build up a share stake in their company.
Open to	Employers running a scheme fix the eligibility rules, usually determined by length of service with the company. Employees may have more than one share option SAYE scheme, provided the overall monthly contribution does not exceed the maximum.
Min–Max	£10 a week minimum; £62.50 a week or £250 a month maximum.
Charges	None.
Withdrawals	No partial withdrawals. Reduced interest rate penalties on early withdrawal; no interest in year one, years two to five, 5 per cent only. If you die, your executor can either take the amount saved or buy shares at the option price.
Interest	Fixed. Including the bonus is equivalent to 5.3 per cent over five years; including the enlarged bonus, the rate over seven years is equivalent to 5.87 per cent. It is accumulated.
Tax	Tax free. Once the share option is exercised, dividends are taxable and there is a potential gains tax liability, based on the actual purchase price of the shares, when you sell them.

HIGH STREET BANKS (AND OTHERS)

Children	No.
How to invest	You will be invited to participate by your employer who must have Inland Revenue approval for the scheme.
Record	Certificate.
Money Mail Rating	***** until the share option is exercised.
Investor protection	Bank compensation scheme covers 90 per cent of savings up to £20,000. Maximum payout £18,000 per person.
Comment	A useful way of hedging your bets. If the company's share rise has risen since you were granted the option, then you exercise the option and buy the share at the lower price fixed when you began savings. You will have a built-in profit. However, if your company has been less successful and the share price is actually lower than the option price, then take the SAYE proceeds as cash.

Tax Exempt Special Savings Account (TESSA)

Tessa is a five year account for either regular or irregular lump savings and provided the capital is left intact for five years, the interest is tax free. If the interest is withdrawn before then, it will be paid net of basic rate tax, but the amount reserved for tax will be paid as a tax-free bonus at the end of the five year period. If the capital is withdrawn before, the interest is taxable. At the end of five years you can transfer your savings into a new TESSA. If you haven't built your first TESSA to the full £9,000 at the end of year five, you can convert that balance to the next five year TESSA and top it up to £9,000 under the TESSA rules.

Suitable for	Erratic lump sum savers, taxpayers and "rainy day" savings.

HIGH STREET BANKS (AND OTHERS)

Open to — Anyone over 18.

Min–Max — Overall maximum over five years, £9,000. Maximum per month £150. Maximum lump sums of £3,000 in year one, £1,800 in years two to four, £600 in year five or up to £1,800 if you have invested less than the maximum in previous years.

Charges — None.

Withdrawals — Interest can be taken net within the five year period. Capital can be withdrawn at any time, but the tax advantages will be lost. At the end of the five year term you must take your tax free "profit" if you reinvest the basic £9,000 into a new TESSA.

Interest — Variable or fixed, usually annual. With some fixed rate schemes, you must deposit your five years saving (less a discount) with them.

Tax — Interest is tax free provided capital is not withdrawn early. If interest net of 20 per cent rate tax is taken during the five year span, the amount reserved for tax will be paid as a tax-free bonus at the end of the term.

Children — No.

Record — Initial certificate and annual update.

Money Mail Rating — *****

Investor protection — Bank compensation scheme covers 90 per cent of savings up to £20,000.

Comment — An attractive and flexible savings vehicle, suitable for second line emergency savings. Tessas may be transferred from one deposit taker to another but this may entail a loss of bonus or a charge. Not all providers allow transfers into their schemes. Compare with rates offered by building societies. Pick a plan with attractive rates but with few or no penalties on transfer out. The evidence to date shows that the main High Street banks' TESSAs have not performed as well as others.

HIGH STREET BANKS (AND OTHERS)

Fixed Term Account

Lump sum, fixed interest rate investment, sometimes described as Fixed Rate Bonds, with money tied up from one month to five years. The interest rate does not necessarily vary with the length of the investment. Escalator Bonds are fixed term investments with a guaranteed higher interest each year.

Suitable for	Anyone taking a view that interest rates elsewhere will fall soon and who wants to lock into fixed rates.
Open to	Anyone.
Min–Max	Minimum commonly £2,000, but can be as little as £500 or as much as £5,000. Usually no maximum.
Charges	None.
Withdrawals	At end of term, other than in exceptional circumstances, but if so the interest rate is usually reduced.
Interest	Fixed higher rates are sometimes negotiable for larger sums. Although fixed for the term, the rates quoted for new deposits change in line with other bank interest rates. For shorter-term investments interest is payable at maturity, otherwise half-yearly or annually. The Co-operative Bank and Lombard North Central allow monthly income.
Tax	Interest is paid net of 20 per cent tax; higher rate taxpayers pay difference of 20 per cent tax more. Banks can pay interest gross to non-taxpayers; non-taxpayers who fail to register will still be able to reclaim the basic rate tax deducted at source.
Children	Not suitable.
How to invest	Interest rates are quoted in bank branches and newspaper advertisements. Apply at a branch, or in writing.
Record	Statement.

HIGH STREET BANKS (AND OTHERS)

Money Mail Rating *****

Investor protection Bank savings compensation scheme covers 90 per cent of savings up to £20,000.

Comment Locking up your money at a fixed rate of interest for a long period is usually inadvisable because of the loss of flexibility. But when interest rates are exceptionally high they could be a bargain. Compare returns with guaranteed income bonds over the same investment time span.

CHAPTER 11

Building Societies

Cash Card Account

Cash card accounts offer an easy withdrawal and deposit system via hole-in-the-wall cash machines and other cash dispensers or automated teller machines (ATMs). Other services, such as standing orders and mini statements, are available in some cases. Originally introduced as an alternative to a cheque book account, in practice more and more societies are adding cheque book facilities to cash card accounts.

Suitable for	Salary transfers. Day-to-day money management for cash, rather than cheque-book oriented customers. Older children, particularly the technology minded.
Open to	Anyone over age 13, sometimes 16.
Min-Max	£1 minimum; no maximum.
Charges	None.
Withdrawals	Up to £100–£250 a day cash from ATMs; larger cheque withdrawals at counter.
Interest	Variable. Account can be tied into either ordinary or instant access accounts and their interest rates and tiers, if relevant, apply. Interest is usually paid half-yearly or annually and accumulated.

BUILDING SOCIETIES

Tax — Interest is paid net of 20 per cent tax; higher rate taxpayers must pay difference of 20 per cent tax more. Building societies can pay interest gross to non-taxpayers; non-taxpayers who fail to register will still be able to reclaim the basic rate tax deducted at source.

Children — Yes, over age 13–16.

How to invest — At a local branch. Larger societies offering this account include Alliance & Leicester, Birmingham Midshires, Bradford & Bingley, Bristol & West, Derbyshire, Halifax.

Record — Passbook if tied to another account, otherwise regular statements (which can be updated at the ATM).

Money Mail Rating — *****

Investor protection — Building society savings compensation scheme covers 90 per cent of savings up to £20,000. Maximum payout £18,000 per depositor.

Comment — Building societies have pushed this account hard as an alternative to much more expensive to administer (from their point of view) cheque book facilities, but are increasingly offering both.

Current Account

Several large societies offer a full cheque-book banking service, including a cheque guarantee card, complete with current account interest. Other societies run cheque book accounts but not with full banking facilities (see High Interest Cheque Accounts). Some of the existing cheque book accounts neither permit overdrafts nor have a cheque guarantee card, but do usually have a credit card link.

Suitable for — Building society current accounts are becoming increasingly competitive with a bank current account and charges tend to be lower.

BUILDING SOCIETIES

Open to — Anyone aged 18 or over.

Min–Max — Varies from £1 minimum up to £100,000 maximum.

Charges — Cheques are usually free unless the account drops below minimum balance, if required. Charges for bounced or stopped cheques. Overdraft interest.

Withdrawals — By cheque, cash on demand up to £250, cash withdrawal machine. Telephone banking facilities available from Alliance & Leicester and Halifax.

Interest — Variable, and sometimes tiered so that the more you have in your account, the more you earn. Interest is usually paid yearly. Northern Rock pay monthly.

Tax — Interest is paid net of 20 per cent tax; 40 per cent higher rate taxpayers pay the difference of 20 per cent tax more. Building societies can pay interest gross to non-taxpayers; non-taxpayers who fail to register will still be able to reclaim the basic rate tax deducted at source.

How to invest — At branches of Britannia, Chelsea, Halifax, Nationwide, Northern Rock, North of England, Norwich & Peterborough and Woolwich. Halifax, Woolwich and Northern Rock will convert to banks in 1997.

Record — Passbook & cheque book stub for additional reference or a monthly bank statement and no passbook.

Money Mail Rating — *****

Investor protection — Building society compensation scheme covers 90 per cent of savings up to £20,000. Maximum payout £18,000 per person.

Comment — Accounts need to be run in conjunction with a credit card to be really effective. Accounts are fully competitive and should be compared with bank interest-bearing current accounts. Which suits you best depends on how you run your financial affairs. Among the building societies Britannia, Chelsea and Northern Rock usually offer good rates.

BUILDING SOCIETIES

Children's Account

Incentive account to attract young people into becoming savers with the help of favourite cartoon characters, gifts, comics, badges, pens and money boxes. Most societies pay their junior members more than the ordinary account rate. There are different accounts for different ages, generally up to 11, and 11 and over.

Suitable for	Pocket money and lump sums and teaching children how to manage their own savings.
Open to	Children up to a stipulated age, most commonly 16 or 18 but sometimes as low as 10. A handful of societies have a lower age limit of five.
Min–Max	£1 minimum; no maximum.
Charges	None.
Withdrawals	On demand from any branch up to £250 cash, cheques up to £5,000. Parent's signature required for withdrawals under the age of seven, occasionally until a child reaches age 10 or 12.
Interest	Variable with wide variations in rates. Some pay a narrow margin over the miserly ordinary share rate while others are much more generous. Interest paid annually or half-yearly and accumulates.
Tax	Building societies can pay interest gross to non-taxpayers, including children. Children must be registered as non-taxpayers by their parents. Forms available in branches.
How to invest	Over 40 societies, including all the major ones, run Children's Accounts. Apply at a local branch.
Record	Passbook. Britannia runs a cash card account for age 11 plus.
Money Mail Rating	*****

BUILDING SOCIETIES

Investor protection
: Building society compensation scheme covers 90 per cent of savings up to £20,000. Maximum payout £18,000 per person.

Comment
: Convenience for school or Saturday leisure activities is the most important aspect of a children's account, and in this respect the building society still scores over the children's bank account which is inaccessible on weekdays during term time. Money-wise kids will appreciate higher interest rates more than the "freebies". Parents should watch the tax trap if money they give to their offspring is invested in a children's account. Tax-free National Savings Certificates or Children's Bonus Bonds would be more appropriate for their regular or substantial money gifts.

    Britannia offers an attractive account with good rates of interest (with card and passbook) for those aged 11–15. Melton Mowbray's Sunny Bond has earned a reputation for good rates for the serious saver (£250 minimum).

Instant Access Account

Building society premium account offering high rates of interest, often on a tiered basis so that the more you invest, the more you earn. A monthly income facility is sometimes included. See also Postal Accounts. An increasing number of societies have launched instant access as "deposit" accounts. Deposit accounts do not confer voting rights in a society.

Suitable for
: Lump sum investments, particularly emergency funds; irregular savings; salary transfers and day-to-day money management.

Open to
: Anyone.

Min–Max
: £500–£1,000, occasionally as little as £1. No maximum.

Charges
: None.

BUILDING SOCIETIES

Withdrawals On demand from any branch, usually up to £250 in cash, £5,000–£15,000 by cheque.

Interest Variable. Rates are tiered so higher balances earn more. Large sums earn $1\frac{1}{4}$–$1\frac{3}{4}$ per cent more than smaller amounts. If the balances drops below minimum level then the ordinary share rate is payable. Interest is usually paid annually, to be accumulated, or paid by cheque or direct into bank or building society account. Monthly income is sometimes available and may be at a slightly lower rate of interest.

Tax Interest is paid net of 20 per cent tax; 40 per cent higher rate taxpayers pay the difference of 20 per cent tax more. Building societies can pay interest gross to non-taxpayers; non-taxpayers who fail to register will still be able to reclaim the basic rate of tax deducted at source.

Children Yes, but parent's signature is required for under-sevens.

How to invest Apply at a branch or agency. Postal service is frequently available.

Record Passbook.

Money Mail Rating *****

Investor protection Building society savings compensation scheme covers 90 per cent of savings up to £20,000. Maximum payout £18,000 per person.

Comment A flexible and versatile account which permits easy switching of funds for those very interested in rates. Check carefully where the trigger points are for the higher interest payments: the first can be as high as £5,000 instead of the more common, and more easily attainable, £2,500. Interest paid half-yearly has a higher compound annual rate if you reinvest the interest. For smaller savers Portman (minimum £500) pays good rates. Alliance & Leicester, to become a bank in 1997, and National & Provincial (now part of the Abbey National banking group) are also usually competitive. As takeovers and mergers become more common among building societies, remember that you need to have been a member for two years to vote (and, in most cases), share in any bonuses, so don't switch accounts needlessly. Deposit accounts can't vote, but are not, under current legislation subject to the two year rule to qualify for bonuses.

High Interest Cheque Account

Interest bearing current account, with a minimum starting sum of £2,000 or £2,500, offered by a handful of societies. Account holders get a cheque book and usually a cash card, cheque guarantee card but no overdraft facility. Standing orders and direct debit facilities are usually available. The interest rate drops dramatically if your balance falls below the usual minimum. Check whether it is a share account, which confers voting rights, or a deposit account which doesn't.

Suitable for	Investors with frequent high value transactions such as school fees and large household bills.
Open to	Anyone aged 18 or over.
Min–Max	Minimum £2,000–£2,500 occasionally, £5,000 more common.
Charges	None.
Withdrawals	By cheque or hole-in-the-wall machines with the cash card.
Interest	Variable and added monthly, quarterly or annually depending on the account. The rates are usually tiered so that the more you have in your account, the more you earn. Expect a derisory rate if your balance falls below the minimum opening balance.
Tax	Interest is paid net of 20 per cent rate tax; 40 per cent higher rate taxpayers pay the difference of 20 per cent tax more. Building societies can pay interest gross to non-taxpayers. Non-taxpayers who fail to register will still be able to reclaim the basic rate tax deducted at source.
Children	No.

How to invest	Apply to High Street branches. Large building societies offering this type of account and with a competitive interest rate record include Bristol & West, Chelsea, Halifax and Alliance & Leicester.
Record	Statement, usually quarterly.
Money Mail Rating	*****
Investor protection	Building society savings compensation scheme covers 90 per cent of savings up to £20,000. Maximum payout £18,000 per person.
Comment	Compare with current accounts on offer from banks and make sure the account is flexible enough to meet your needs. Chelsea runs its Classic Account through the post.

Monthly Income Account

Lump sum investment which pays interest monthly and which is usually linked to either an instant access, notice account, postal account or term account (see pages 53, 57 and 60). Some societies pay the same rates of interest in which case the compound annual rate (CAR) is higher; others trim the interest marginally because it is paid monthly.

Suitable for	Retired persons (but check the age allowance trap, see page 31) and others, such as non-working mothers, who need monthly income.
Open to	Anyone.
Min–Max	£2,000–£2,500 although occasionally lower. No maximum.
Charges	None.
Withdrawals	Same as for underlying account.

BUILDING SOCIETIES

Interest	Variable, paid monthly either by cheque or direct to bank or other building society account. Halifax offers a fixed rate for one year.
Tax	Interest paid net of 20 per cent tax; 40 per cent higher rate taxpayers pay the difference of 20 per cent tax more. Gross interest available for registered non-taxpayers.
Children	Not suitable.
How to invest	Most societies have monthly income accounts. Apply at a branch. Postal service is frequently available.
Record	Passbook; half-yearly or annual statements as well in some cases.
Money Mail Rating	*****
Investor protection	Building society savings compensation scheme covers 90 per cent of savings up to £20,000. Maximum payout £18,000 per person.
Comment	Shop around: interest rates and thresholds for higher interest rates on tiered accounts vary. Check the compound annual rate (CAR), particularly if you plan to reinvest rather than spend the income. Compare with National Savings Income Bonds, Pensioners Guaranteed Income Bond (for ages 65 and over) and Guaranteed Income Bonds. Top rates from building societies are usually available on term shares but instant access postal accounts run by Bradford & Bingley and Cheltenham & Gloucester offer good rates.

Notice Account

Lump sum investment account which requires notice of from seven days to one, two or three months to withdraw funds. With accounts needing notice of one month or more, investors have the option of loss of interest for relevant period and instant access. Accounts are usually tiered so that the more you have invested, the more you earn. Monthly income is usually available.

Suitable for	Lump sum investments needed at a specific future date and longer-term investments.
Open to	Anyone.
Min–Max	£500–£1,000 minimum; no maximum.
Charges	None.
Withdrawals	Any amount after required notice period, or instant access if you accept loss of interest for relevant notice period. This option is not always available on seven day notice accounts. If you keep a balance, usually of £10,000, instant withdrawal from the surplus is allowed.
Interest	Variable, usually paid annually to be accumulated or paid by cheque or direct into another account, or paid as monthly income. Larger investors earn 1.2–2 per cent more than smaller investors.
Tax	Interest is paid net of 20 per cent tax; 40 per cent higher rate taxpayers pay the difference of 20 per cent tax more. Gross interest is available for registered non-taxpayers.
Children	Yes. Particularly for their long-term savings. Parent's signature is required for under-sevens.
How to invest	Most societies have notice accounts. Apply at a branch. Postal service is frequently available.
Record	Passbook.
Money Mail Rating	*****
Investor protection	Building society savings compensation scheme covers 90 per cent of savings up to £20,000. Maximum payout £18,000 per person.

Comment	Rates vary widely between societies and you can get up to 2 per cent more before tax by choosing the right society. Coventry and Yorkshire are often among the best payers on 90 day accounts. Check the compound annual rate if interest is paid monthly. When interest rates are fluctuating, give your relevant notice immediately you make an investment in order to be able to switch funds quickly if a better interest rate opportunity appears. You are not bound to it if you change your mind.

Ordinary or Share Account

The basic no-strings, no-extras building society account offering easy access and miserly interest rates should be avoided. Opt for an instant access account with a low minimum balance instead.

Suitable for	It is hard to make a case for anyone. These accounts are very much the poor relation in the range.
Open to	Anyone.
Min–Max	£1. No maximum.
Charges	None.
Withdrawals	On demand from any branch or agency up to £250 in cash; by cheque from branches up to £5,000.
Interest	Variable; paid half-yearly to be accumulated or paid by cheque or direct into a bank or other building society account.
Tax	Interest is paid net of 20 per cent tax; 40 per cent higher rate taxpayers pay the difference of 20 per cent tax more. Building societies can pay interest gross to non-taxpayers; non-taxpayers who fail to register will still be able to reclaim the basic rate of tax deducted at source.
Children	Yes, but parent's signature is required for under-sevens.

BUILDING SOCIETIES

How to invest	At a local branch or agency.
Record	Passbook.
Money Mail Rating	*****
Investor protection	Building society compensation scheme covers 90 per cent of savings up to £20,000. Maximum payout £18,000 per person.
Comment	Increasingly obsolete account. Use Nationwide's Cashbuilder account, an instant access account with minimum opening balance of £1. Once you reach £100–£250 the choice gets wider with Leeds & Holbeck and National & Provincial. Children's Accounts frequently pay more to young savers irrespective of balance. Use this account for a springboard to Instant Access Account as soon as your savings reach the minimum investment for this account.

Postal Account

A growing number of building societies operate accounts which are run exclusively through the post rather than the branch network. They offer attractive interest rates for those willing to operate the account using the first class post rather than a local branch. You can usually get your money back on demand but allow a couple of days for the post. Check that it is a share account which confers voting rights.

Suitable for	Anyone looking for good returns who is happy to run their account outside the High Street.
Open to	Anyone.
Min–Max	£1,000–£2,500; no maximum.
Charges	None.
Withdrawals	At any time on instructions sent via the post. The society provides paying-in and withdrawal slips. Some postal accounts, such as Chelsea's, offer a cheque book.

Interest	Variable and tiered so that the more you have in your account, the more you earn. Interest is usually paid annually or monthly.
Tax	Interest is paid net of 20 per cent tax; 40 per cent higher rate taxpayers pay the difference of 20 per cent tax more. Building societies can pay interest gross to non-taxpayers; non-taxpayers who fail to register will still be able to reclaim the basic rate of tax deducted at source.
Children	Yes, parents operate the account.
How to invest	Through the post. Cheltenham & Gloucester allow you to open an account through their branch network, but thereafter it must be run through the post. Societies offering good postal accounts include Birmingham Midshires, Bradford & Bingley, Chelsea (with cheque book), Cheltenham & Gloucester, Britannia and Northern Rock. Other societies to watch which sometimes offer good accounts include Leeds & Holbeck, Norwich & Peterborough, Nottingham and Scarborough. Bristol and West now operate a telephone dealing service. You can also operate Cheltenham & Gloucester and Bradford & Bingley accounts by telephone.
Record	Regular statements.
Money Mail Rating	*****
Investor protection	Building society compensation scheme covers 90 per cent of savings up to £20,000. Maximum payout £18,000 per person.
Comment	Cheltenham & Gloucester, now part of Lloyds Bank, has traditionally paid good rates on its account, and so does Bradford & Bingley and Bristol & West. Postal accounts are the new flagship accounts for buildings societies. Watch out for new entries into the field as they tend to come out with very competitive rates.

BUILDING SOCIETIES

Regular Savings Account

Regular monthly savings scheme for unlimited period paying investors a higher rate of interest than on an ordinary account. One withdrawal a year is sometimes allowed, so is one month's savings lapse. It is usually possible to vary the amount saved.

Suitable for	Short-to-medium savings goals, such as a holiday, and more particularly a house.
Open to	Anyone.
Min–Max	£1–£10 a month minimum; £100–£250 maximum (doubled for joint accounts).
Charges	None.
Withdrawals	Partial withdrawals once or twice a year may be permitted, otherwise the account is closed or transferred to an ordinary account.
Interest	Variable, paid half-yearly or annually and usually accumulated in the account. The rate is 1–1½ per cent above the ordinary rate.
Tax	Interest is paid net of 20 per cent tax; 40 per cent higher rate taxpayers pay the difference of 20 per cent tax more. Building societies can pay interest gross to non-taxpayers; non-taxpayers who fail to register will still be able to reclaim the basic rate of tax deducted at source.
Children	Not suitable.
How to invest	Most societies offer a regular savings scheme; apply at a branch.
Record	Passbook.
Money Mail Rating	*****

BUILDING SOCIETIES

Investor protection Building society savings compensation scheme covers 90 per cent of savings up to £20,000. Maximum payout £18,000 per person.

Comment With a couple of exceptions, interest rates on these accounts are not at the top of the building society range, so savers should use the account as a stepping stone to building up sufficient capital to transfer to a higher-paying instant access account. Nationwide and Bradford & Bingley now have competitive regular savings schemes.

Save As You Earn (SAYE)

2nd Issue

(Withdrawn November 1994 Budget)

Regular monthly savings scheme for five years with option to leave investment for further two. Interest, which accumulates, is tax free and there is a bonus equivalent to 14 months' payments, tax free, at the end of five years, or 28 months' if you leave the savings in for the next two years. A gap of six months' savings can be made up. Current savers should continue with the plan.

Charges None.

Withdrawals No partial withdrawals; repayment takes two to three weeks. Reduced interest rate penalties on early withdrawals: no interest in year one, years two to five interest of 6 per cent only (8 per cent if you die).

Interest Fixed. Including the bonus, the rate is equivalent to 8.3 per cent a year over five years; including the enlarged bonus, the rate over seven years is equivalent to 8.62 per cent a year. It accumulates and is paid out when the contract matures.

Tax Tax free.

Children No.

Money Mail Rating	*****
Investor protection	Building society savings compensation scheme covers 90 per cent of savings up to £20,000.
Comment	Keep up the savings for five years; early surrender rates are unattractive. Worth holding on to.

Save As You Earn (SAYE)

Series "F" Share Option Scheme

Regular monthly savings linked to a company share option scheme. Employees are offered the option to buy shares at a price fixed at the start of the five-year savings period which cannot be less than 80 per cent of market value. Employees invest a set amount each month in the SAYE scheme. At the end of five years they can either use the money to exercise the share option or take the money with a bonus; they can leave the money invested for another two years to obtain a higher bonus BUT they will then lose the share option entitlement. However, some employers offer a seven-year share option plan when the share option can then be exercised.

Interest in the SAYE accumulates tax free. In addition there is a bonus of 9 months' payments tax free at the end of five years, or 18 months' if you leave the savings in for the next two years.

Suitable for	Employees who want to build up a share stake in their company.
Open to	Employers running a scheme fix the eligibility rules, usually determined by length of service with the company. Employees may have more than one share option SAYE scheme, provided the overall monthly contribution does not exceed the maximum.
Min–Max	£10 a week minimum; £62.50 a week or £250 a month maximum.
Charges	None.

BUILDING SOCIETIES

Withdrawals — No partial withdrawals. Reduced interest rate penalties on early withdrawal; no interest in year one; years two to five, 5 per cent. If you die, your executor can either take the amount saved or buy shares at the option price.

Interest — Fixed. Including the bonus, interest is equivalent to 5.3 per cent over five years; including the enlarged bonus, the rate over seven years is equivalent to 5.87 per cent. It is accumulated.

Tax — Tax free. Once the share option is exercised, dividends are taxable and there is a potential gains tax liability, based on the actual purchase price of the shares, when you sell them.

Children — No.

How to invest — You will be invited to participate by your employer who must have Inland Revenue approval for the scheme.

Record — Certificate.

Money Mail Rating — ***** until the share option is exercised.

Investor protection — Building societies compensation scheme covers 90 per cent of savings up to £20,000. Maximum payout £18,000 per person.

Comment — A useful way of hedging your bets. If the company's shares have risen since you were granted the option, then you exercise the option and buy the share at the lower price fixed when you began saving. You will have a built-in profit. However, if your company has been less successful and the share price is actually lower than the option price, then take the SAYE proceeds as cash.

BUILDING SOCIETIES

Tax Exempt Special Savings Account (TESSA)

TESSA is a five year account for either regular or irregular lump sum savings and provided the capital is left intact for five years, the interest is tax free. If the interest is withdrawn before then, it will be paid net of basic rate tax, but the amount reserved for tax will be paid as a tax-free bonus at the end of the five year period. If the capital is withdrawn before, the interest is taxable. At the end of the five years you can transfer your savings into a new TESSA. If you haven't built up your first TESSA to the full £9,000 at the end of year five, you can convert that balance to the next five year TESSA and top it up to £9,000 under the TESSA rules.

Suitable for	Erratic lump sum savers, taxpayers and "rainy day" savings.
Open to	Anyone over 18.
Min–Max	Overall maximum over five years, £9,000. Maximum per month £150. Maximum lump sum £3,000 in year one, £1,800 in years two to four, £600 in year five or up to £1,800 if the maximum has not been invested in previous years.
Charges	None.
Withdrawals	Interest can be taken net within the five year period. Capital can be taken at any time, but tax advantages will be lost. At the end of the five year term you must take your tax free "profit" if you reinvest the basic £9,000 into a new TESSA.
Interest	Variable, usually annually.
Tax	Interest is tax free provided capital is not withdrawn early. If net interest is taken during the five year span, the amount reserved for tax will be paid as a tax-free bonus at the end of the term.
Children	No.
Record	Initial certificate and annual update.

Money Mail Rating	*****
Investor protection	Building society savings compensation scheme covers 90 per cent of savings up to £20,000.
Comment	An attractive and flexible savings vehicle, suitable for second level emergency savings. Tessas may be transferred from one financial institution to another but this may entail a loss of bonus or a charge. Not all providers allow transfers into their scheme. Pick a plan with attractive rates and no transfer penalties. Alliance & Leicester and Yorkshire are two large societies which have, to date, offered consistently competitive rates. Compare with plans on offer from banks and other deposit takers.

Fixed Term Share

Lump sum investment of renewed popularity, sometimes called Fixed Rate Bond. Investors' funds are locked in for a period – the term – of one to five years, although withdrawals are sometimes permitted with a loss of interest penalty. Interest rates are at the high end of the building society range, and often include a guaranteed differential over ordinary rate. In a period of low interest rates, building societies are anxious to tie in savers with term shares. In response to competition from National Savings Pensioners Guaranteed Income Bond interest rates are becoming more attractive. Escalator Bonds are fixed term investments with a guaranteed higher interest rate each year.

Suitable for	Relatively large lump sums. Top rates paid on sums as large as £100,000. Anyone taking a view on interest rates and wants to look in at current levels.
Open to	Anyone.
Min–Max	£1,000–£2,000 minimum; no maximum.
Charges	None.

BUILDING SOCIETIES

Withdrawals — Usually not allowed. Capital plus interest earned to date is repaid on death within the term.

Interest — Fixed, paid annually, half-yearly or rolled up to maturity.

Tax — Interest is paid net of 20 per cent tax; 40 per cent higher rate taxpayers must pay the difference of 20 per cent tax more. Building societies can pay interest gross to non-taxpayers; non-taxpayers who fail to register will still be able to reclaim the basic rate of tax deducted at source.

Children — Yes.

How to invest — Apply at branches or by post or through newspaper advertisements.

Record — Passbook or certificate.

Money Mail Rating — *****

Investor protection — Building society savings compensation scheme covers 90 per cent of savings up to £20,000. Maximum payout £18,000 per person.

Comment — Always check the withdrawal options. Fixed interest term shares can be attractive when interest rates are falling, however. The guaranteed differential above the ordinary share rate can be less generous than it sounds, as ordinary share rates tend to rise more slowly and fall further than other account rates. With escalator bonds check the average yield over the term (usually five years).

CHAPTER 12

Gold

Gold Coins

Gold coins are the easiest and most reliable way for a private investor to take a direct stake in gold. As a coin it is a non-income producing asset, it is held either purely for speculation that the price of gold, which can fluctuate considerably, will rise; or for the simple pleasure of owning it. The modern coins contain one Troy ounce of gold but stand at a premium to the price of gold, quoted in dollars per ounce. Popular coins include South African Krugerrands, the Canadian Maple Leaf and the Chinese Panda. The UK began minting a new gold coin, the Britannia, in 1987.

Suitable for	At the most 5 per cent to 10 per cent of savings and then only out of capital which will not be required at short notice. Alternative to cash gifts.
Open to	Anyone.
Min–Max	Current price of one gold coin – £215–£216, February 1997; – or less for Sovereigns which contain 0.2354 Troy oz gold – £50–£52, February 1997. No maximum.
Charges	Commission included in price of coin; 17.5 per cent VAT charged on all coins bought in the UK (except those more than 100 years old, where VAT is charged on the dealer's profit margins only). Coins

GOLD

bought and held in the Channel Islands or Gibraltar are not subject to VAT, but attract a storage charge of typically £2 a coin and an annual service fee of 50p per half-year, paid in arrears.

Withdrawals At current market price, immediately.

Tax Capital gains tax liability on profits except for pre-1838 Sovereigns.

Children Gifts.

How to invest Check prices, quoted in dollars, in newspaper. Most banks buy and sell gold coins but usually impose a minimum of 10 coins/£3,000. Compare prices charged by dealers. A full coin dealing (and storage if required) service is available from Braid & Co, Gold Investments Ltd and Spink & Son Ltd. If you deal through the Channel Islands and keep the coins there to avoid VAT, stick to subsidiaries of well-known UK banks.

Record If you hold the coins yourself, none. If coins are held offshore, certificate and regular statement.

Money Mail Rating *!!!! to !!!!!

Investor protection Gold coins fall outside the scope of the Financial Services Act; in the UK store coins at bank; if coins are kept in the Channel Islands, make sure the coins are physically held in your name.

Comment A limited exposure to gold can be very rewarding, particularly at times of international political uncertainty or strong currency fluctuations. However, it is worth noting that the gold price did not surge ahead in the Gulf War, as might have been expected. A platinum coin, the Isle of Man Noble, is also available, and in several denominations.

CHAPTER 13

Friendly Society

Regular Savings Policy

A regular savings scheme, with contributions paid monthly, half yearly or annually, for a 10-year period. It is a form of life assurance contract invested in a tax-free investment fund; at least half the premium income is to be invested in fixed interest investments such as Government securities or building societies. The remainder is often invested in unit trusts. Friendly society rules were relaxed at the beginning of 1997 and friendly societies are expected to offer more conventional life insurance in future (see Chapter Fourteen).

Suitable for	Regular savings for yourself or for a child which you are sure you can maintain; higher rate taxpayers.
Open to	Anyone aged 18 or over.
Min–Max	A minimum of £10 a month or £100 a year. A maximum of £25 a month or £270 a year. Each person is only permitted one policy in all. Married couples each take one out. Existing policyholders will be able to increase their premium when new limits come into force.
Charges	Built into your premium.
Withdrawals	If you withdraw your funds before the end of the 10-year term then you will receive a return of

FRIENDLY SOCIETY

contributions only. After 10 years the policy proceeds can be withdrawn or left to earn interest. On death within 10 years guaranteed life cover of £750 to £1,000 is paid out.

Interest   Variable. It is reinvested.

Tax   Proceeds are free of income and capital gains tax.

Children   Investment can be made on behalf of a child with a maximum of one policy per child.

How to invest   Obtain application forms from a friendly society such as Family, Homeowners, Liverpool Victoria, Manchester Unity, Time Assurance and Tunbridge Wells.

Record   Insurance Policy.

Money Mail Rating   ****!

Comment   There is no point in taking out such a contract unless it stays in force for 10 years; building society linked schemes offer better value. Plans linked to unit trusts are inflexible compared with regular savings into units via either a unit trust regular savings (effectively free of capital gains tax) scheme or a personal equity plan (free of capital gains tax). Larger premium policies are partly invested in conventional life assurance funds which do not roll up tax-free.

CHAPTER 14

Life Insurance

Annuity

A lump sum investment which cannot be redeemed, in return for which investors receive an income for life. The amount payable will depend upon your age: the older you are, the better the return. The interest paid is usually fixed at the outset. Annuity contracts can be varied to provide an income which continues until the surviving spouse dies, or a guaranteed income which continues for five or 10 years regardless of whether the annuitant survives. This form of annuity is known as a purchased annuity and is not to be confused with a Pension Annuity (see page **74**).

Suitable for	Older men and women; fixed income offers little protection against rising costs in periods of high inflation.
Open to	Anyone, in theory, but rarely worthwhile for people under 70 (men) or 75 (women).
Min–Max	Minimum realistic level is around £1,000 – producing (at January 1997) around £114 p.a. income for men aged 65 and £92 for women aged 60. No maximum.
Charges	Built into the contract terms.
Withdrawals	None.

Interest	Fixed, according to each type of annuity. A few unit-linked contracts provide rising interest from a much lower starting base. Interest is usually paid in arrears by cheque or direct to a bank account monthly, quarterly, half-yearly or annually.
Tax	Part of the annuity is treated as return of capital and is tax free, the remainder is treated as income and has basic rate tax deducted at source. Non-taxpayers can be paid gross; higher rate taxpayers pay more.
Children	Not suitable.
How to invest	Most life insurance companies offer annuities. Check rates in specialist publications such as *Money Management* or *Planned Savings* and/or consult an insurance broker.
Record	Annuity contract, setting out the terms.
Money Mail Rating	*****
Investor protection	Policyholders' protection scheme covers 90 per cent of benefits.
Comment	With modest inflation only, annuities can be worthwhile for the more elderly. They can also be useful for inheritance tax planning for people with large estates. Older men and women owning their own property can release some of the capital "tied up" in the house with the use of Income Plan, based upon an annuity and mortgage package.

Pension Annuity

If your pension arrangements have been made through either a self-employed retirement plan or a personal pension plan (see pages 126–127), your income in retirement will come from a pension annuity. You are not obliged to take your pension annuity with the same insurance company which provided the pension plan, but can use the open-market option to select a higher paying pension annuity from another insurance company.

Suitable for	It is the only option for men and women who have saved for their pension with either a retirement or personal pension plan.
Open to	Anyone in the above categories from age 60–75, although in certain cases pension annuities may be taken earlier.
Min–Max	None. It depends on the amount of money built up in your pension fund or "pot".
Charges	Built into the contract terms.
Withdrawals	A cash lump sum can be taken at retirement. With self-employed retirement annuities the tax free cash ranges, for a man, from 24 per cent of the pension fund at age 60 to 30 per cent at age 70. For a woman, the tax free lump sum would be 22 per cent at age 60 rising to 28 per cent at 70. With a personal pension, the tax free sum is restricted to 25 per cent of the pension fund for both men and women.
Interest	Fixed. Can be made monthly, quarterly, half yearly or annually in arrears. If income is taken monthly in advance, a slightly lower annuity rate will apply.
Tax	The annuity income is taxed at the pensioner's individual tax rate.
Children	No.
How to invest	If you stay with your pension provider, then the transfer to pension annuity will be done for you; an independent financial adviser who specialises in annuities will advise on the open-market option.
Record	Annuity contract.
Money Mail Rating	*****
Investor Protection	Policyholders' protection scheme covers 90 per cent of benefits.

Comment	It is important to investigate the open-market option at retirement. Annuity rates from one insurance company to another can vary by as much as 20–30 per cent – which can make a lot of difference to the amount of income you can enjoy at retirement.

Flexible Annuity

This variation of the Pension Annuity was introduced in 1995–96 in order to protect people coming up to retirement at a time when annuity rates were low. Instead of investing the money built up in a personal pension fund immediately in a pension annuity at retirement, the purchase of the annuity can be deferred until age 75. However, 35 per cent of the income that an annuity would have provided is taken as income from the pension fund in the meantime.

Suitable for	Men and women approaching retirement at a time when annuity rates are low.
Open to	People who have saved for their retirement through a personal pension plan, and are under age 75. Anyone with a retirement annuity plan must first convert that into a personal pension plan.
Min–Max	None. Depends on the size of the individual's pension fund at retirement.
Charges	Built into the contract.
Withdrawals	See Pension Annuity (page 74) for details of the tax free cash lump sum that can be taken immediately at retirement. An income of 35 per cent of the level of income that would have been provided by the annuity must be taken from the pension fund. The balance of the pension fund must be transferred into a pension annuity no later than by age 75.
Interest	Interest on the first set of income from the pension fund is related to annuity rates at retirement. Income from the annuity taken at 75 (or earlier if annuity rates are attractive) will depend on annuity rates at that time.

LIFE INSURANCE

Tax — Lump sum at retirement is tax free; income taken thereafter is subject to income tax.

Children — No.

How to invest — If you are keeping your pension arrangements with the company where you did your pensions savings, it will organise your flexible annuity. Use the services of an independent financial adviser specialising in annuities if you want to use the open-market option.

Record — Insurance policy followed by annuity.

Money Mail Rating — ****! until the annuity is purchased, then *****.

Comment — Flexible annuities are a valuable option. In the early 'nineties, for example, annuity rates fell by as much as 30 per cent – which meant a much lower income for someone retiring then. There is some scope for inheritance tax planning with a joint life annuity.

Distribution Bond

This is an important type of Investment Bond. It is a lump sum investment into a mainstream single premium life insurance policy which is the standard mix of gilt-edged securities, shares both in the UK and overseas, and property. The main difference between it and a conventional investment bond is that instead of rolling the income up in the life fund, the managers distribute it to investors, usually half-yearly. In addition it is possible to top up the income from capital.

Suitable for — Higher rate taxpayers and older people who need to augment their retirement income, particularly those who near the ceiling for age allowance, the extra tax allowance given to those on modest income aged 65 years or more.

Open to — It varies from company to company, but age 14 to 80 are common limits.

LIFE INSURANCE

Min–Max	Varies. Ranges from £2,500 to £100,000, but £5,000 to £50,000 are more typical limits.
Charges	An initial fee, commonly of 5 per cent, is deducted from the initial investment; there is also an annual fee of 1–1.5 per cent.
Interest	Variable; most managers aim to provide rising income; it is possible to use a tax-efficient "withdrawal" facility which enables investors to withdraw a certain amount of capital to top up income. Provided no more than 5 per cent is withdrawn, it is tax free to basic rate taxpayers while higher rate taxpayers can defer their tax liability (on the difference between the 23 per cent basic rate and 40 per cent higher rate band) for twenty years. The assumption is that by that time, many bondholders will have retired and no longer be 40 per cent rate taxpayers, and therefore will not have to pay any tax after all. This concession is currently being reviewed by the Inland Revenue.
Tax	Income tax and capital gains tax on realised gains are paid by the insurance company and are thus reflected in the underlying unit price. The proceeds are tax free for basic rate taxpayers; non-taxpayers cannot reclaim any income tax paid; higher rate taxpayers must pay more. A higher rate taxpayer's liability is reduced by "top-slicing". This averages the profit over the number of years the bond was held to arrive at the taxable amount.
Children	Yes, if age limits permit.
How to invest	Buy direct from an insurance company; use the services of an independent financial adviser to find the one most suitable for your needs.
Record	Insurance policy.
Money Mail Rating	**!!! to ****!
Investor protection	Policyholders' Protection Act covers 90 per cent of your savings.

LIFE INSURANCE

Comment These are conservatively managed investments, with a record of rising income (from investments rather than capital withdrawal). However, the bond is more heavily taxed internally than unit and investment trusts. They are likely to show a steady rather than volatile investment performance.

Guaranteed Income Bond and Guaranteed Growth Bond

A lump sum investment with a fixed return over a term of one to five years (commonly), sometimes six to 10 years and, rarely, as long as 15 years. If the bond pays out the interest, it is an Income Bond; if the income is accumulated, it is a Growth Bond. Underlying investments linked to fixed rate investments.

Suitable for Augmenting retirement income (but check the age allowance, see page 31); building up capital before retirement; specific savings target (Growth Bonds); taking a view on interest rates.

Open to Minimum age is often 16 or 18; maximum age is commonly 80 or 85, occasionally 90.

Min–Max Minimum £1,000–£2,000. Maximum none, or £50,000, £75,000 or £100,000.

Charges Built into contract terms.

Withdrawals At maturity, original investment – Income Bonds; guaranteed value – Growth Bonds; early surrender values, if available, are usually poor. Death benefits: original investment – Income Bonds; original investment plus 6–9 per cent – Growth Bonds.

Interest Fixed. Income Bonds pay monthly (the rate is usually marginally lower), half-yearly and most commonly annually. Interest accumulates with Growth Bonds.

Tax Interest is paid net of tax (Growth and Income Bonds alike) which usually cannot be reclaimed by non-taxpayers; higher rate taxpayers pay more.

LIFE INSURANCE

Children	Not suitable.
How to invest	Some bonds are only available for a limited period – check newspapers for offers. Check rates in specialist publications such as *Money Management* or *Planned Savings* and/or consult a financial adviser or insurance broker. Stick to UK insurance companies.
Record	Insurance policy.
Money Mail Rating	*****
Investor protection	Policyholders' protection scheme covers 90 per cent of benefits agreed by UK insurance companies, provided they are not excessive.
Comment	High fixed returns are attractive if you think interest rates will fall. Insurance companies carefully "match" their underlying investments to provide the guaranteed return at a set date; but the guarantee is still only as good as the company issuing it, so always choose an authorised UK insurance company. Policies sold by an overseas life insurance company which is not authorised in the UK are not included in the policyholders' protection scheme.

Guaranteed Stock Market or Equity Bond

This the most novel form of investment bond yet. The basic insurance bond (see page **83**) is a lump sum investment into a single premium insurance policy, either With Profits or Managed linked to the stock market. The Guaranteed Stock Market Bond goes one stage further by letting you benefit from the gains on the stock market at the same time as shielding you from potential losses. The bond's life is usually limited to five years. Companies offering these bonds in effect insure against the risk of falling markets by using sophisticated investment tools known as "derivatives" or futures and options.

But the cost of protecting investors against a stock market fall has to be paid for. This normally means giving up the income from your investment. A bond will normally promise to match some or all of the capital growth of the market,

LIFE INSURANCE

even if subsequently it were to fall, but in return you sacrifice any income the bond might have earned. Guaranteed Stock Market Bonds sound a lot more complicated than they actually are.

Suitable for	Cautious investors. Once your investment has achieved a certain level, that gain will be locked in and cannot be taken away. It is conceivable that you might not make money if the stock market were to go into decline, but nor would you lose it either. They are not recommended for people needing income.
Open to	Varies according to company; 14 to 80 years of age are the most extreme limits.
Min–Max	Varies. £1,000 is a common minimum.
Charges	Initial fees of around 5 per cent and an annual fee of 1–1.5 per cent.
Withdrawals	Not recommended until maturity.
Interest	None.
Tax	The insurance company pays income tax and capital gains tax on realised gains, which is reflected in the underlying unit price. The proceeds are tax free for basic rate taxpayers; higher rate taxpayers must pay more.
Children	Yes, if age limits permit.
How to invest	Direct from a company (these bonds are heavily advertised in the press), or use the services of an independent financial adviser for a recommendation from a selection of bonds. TSB and Save & Prosper are big players in this field
Record	A policy which looks like an investment certificate.
Money Mail Rating	****!
Investor Protection	Policyholders' Protection Act covers 90 per cent of the unit value.

81

LIFE INSURANCE

Comment — The bonds are a half-way house between depositing your money and earning interest and having a go on the stock market. But you are reliant entirely on capital growth for your return, as income has been sacrificed for the guarantee against losses.

High Income Bond

A lump sum investment which offers an above-average net income, but unlike Guaranteed Income Bonds there is no guarantee that you will get your capital back when the bond matures. The performance of these bonds is normally linked to a stock market index usually the FT–SE 100 (which tracks the top 100 companies quoted on the Stock Exchange). If this does not fall during the life of the bond, usually five years, then you will get your money back. If it does fall below, then you may lose some of your capital. In these circumstances, you will get back your original capital minus the value of the income you've had in the meantime.

Suitable for — Anyone seeking to boost their income, although they are not recommended for an investor's entire portfolio. They are high particularly suitable for higher rate taxpayers, but the high level of income paid means that non-taxpayers should not rule them out, even though they cannot reclaim any tax.

Open to — Usually to anyone between the age 14 and 80.

Min–Max — Minimum varies, but £1,000 is typical.

Charges — Initial fee, usually of 5 per cent and annual of 1–1.5 per cent.

Interest — In March 1996 rates were 9–10 per cent net of basic rate tax.

Withdrawals — Not recommended until maturity.

Tax — The insurance company pays income and capital gains tax on the fund's investments. Income is paid to investors net of basic rate tax which cannot be reclaimed, although higher rate taxpayers must pay more.

Children — Yes, if age limits permits, but rarely suitable for them.

How to invest	Direct from an insurance company (these bonds are heavily advertised in the press) of use the services of an independent financial adviser.
Record	A policy which looks more like an investment certificate.
Money Mail Rating	****!
Investor Protection	Policyholders' Protection Act covers 90 per cent of the unit value.
Comment	The high return is attractive but you could lose some of the "face" value of your capital if stock markets fall. Most insurance companies now measure the performance of the stock market(s) over the last three/six months of the bond's life in order to protect savers against a sudden drop in the market. But investors should check carefully all the capital repayment rules. Make sure you understand what you are buying – there is concern that investors do not realise that if the stock market falls by over a certain amount they will only get the *balance* of their capital back – less the income they've received, and probably spent!

Managed Bond

A lump sum investment in the form of a single-premium life insurance policy linked directly to an individual market sector, or mixture of different types of investment. There are investment bonds linked to UK equities, international equities, fixed interest stock, cash, convertible stock and property (Property Bond), both in the UK or overseas. Other bonds are linked to a mixture of some or all of these investment categories. Investors can switch to one category from another in the same group without cashing in the policy.

Suitable for	Higher rate taxpayers and older people on modest incomes who are borderline cases in respect of the age allowance (see page **31**), the extra tax relief given to some people over the age of 65.
Open to	Varies; anyone, usually from 14 to 80 years of age.
Min–Max	£500, commonly £1,000 and sometimes £2,500 minimum. No maximum.

Charges	An initial fee of typically 5 per cent is deducted from the initial investment; annual fee of 1–1.5 per cent.
Withdrawals	On demand, at current market value; on death current market value of units (more in earlier years).
Interest	Variable; accumulated within the fund. Up to 5 per cent of original investment can be withdrawn as "income" with income tax liability (applicable to higher rate taxpayers only) deferred until the bond is finally encashed, or after 20 years. "Income" withdrawal does not have to be declared on your tax return. This concession is currently being reviewed by the Inland Revenue.
Tax	Income tax and capital gains tax apply to realised gains paid by the insurance company, reflected in the underlying unit price. The proceeds are tax free for basic rate taxpayers; non-taxpayers cannot reclaim any income tax paid; higher rate taxpayers must pay more. A higher rate taxpayer's liability is reduced by "top-slicing" which averages the gain over the number of years the bond was held.
Children	Yes, where age limits permit.
How to invest	Check the performance of underlying units in specialist publications such as *Money Management* or *Planned Savings*; phone or write for details from insurance companies before investing.
Record	Insurance policy.
Money Mail Rating	****! to *!!!!
Investor protection	Policyholders' protection scheme covers 90 per cent of current unit value.
Comment	This bond's internal capital gains tax liability is a major disadvantage compared with lump sum investment in unit trusts which roll up without capital gains tax. "Income" withdrawal is beneficial to higher rate taxpayers who can defer tax liability

until retirement when their tax bracket is likely to be lower; older people will not have their age allowance entitlement jeopardised by "income" withdrawal.

School Fees Educational Trust

A lump sum investment via a trust into a life insurance company for a child which will pay school fees on either a flat or increasing basis. It can be taken out immediately before the fees become due, or up to 13 years in advance. It is not essential to identify the school in advance, and you can change your mind and surrender the policy instead. Regular savings are sometimes permitted if the policy is taken out at least three years ahead of first fee. The future of these trusts is in doubt following an Inland Revenue decision to stop giving them tax relief. This is still under review, although it has now been established that existing school fee trusts will not be affected.

Suitable for	Parents, grandparents and any adult wishing to fund school fees in advance, particularly higher rate tax-payers.
Open to	Anyone.
Min–Max	Depends on the size of fees and the number of years ahead they are required. Minimum £500–£2,500; £50 a month; no maximum.
Charges	Built into the contract.
Withdrawals	Paid as agreed termly fees; if the child dies, 95–100 per cent of the original purchase price plus interest is returned; otherwise non-guaranteed surrender value.
Interest	Fixed; accumulated within the trust.
Tax	The fees from the trust are paid tax free as the person making the payment has no legal interest in the policy.
Children	Improbable – the trust is for their benefit.
How to invest	Equitable Life (which accepts monthly and irregular lump sum contributions), Royal Life, Save & Prosper, and School Fees Insurance Agency (SFIA) all have educational trust facilities.

Record	Contract with trust.
Money Mail Rating	*****
Investor protection	Policyholders' protection scheme covers 90 per cent of benefits.
Comment	More flexible than investing school fees in advance via a "composition fee" scheme direct with the school of your choice. The earlier the school fee investment is made, the smaller the capital outlay. Don't make an investment until the trusts' tax position has been finally clarified.

Traded Endowment Policies

A lump sum invested which is growing in popularity. These are sometimes known as "second-hand" endowment policies – which is exactly what they are. People who no longer wish to keep their With-Profits Endowment Policies (see page 89) running traditionally had the option of surrendering them for a low value or making them paid up. A third option is now becoming widely used: redundant policies can be sold and assigned to other people at a price which is often significantly higher than the policy's surrender value.

Investors who buy second-hand policies enjoy the benefits of a long term with-profits policy without having to wait, say, 25 years to gain from it. There is the guaranteed lump sum assured plus all the accrued bonuses built up over the years and no great exposure to stock market fluctuations. The buyer keeps paying the premiums but all the initial costs have been borne by the original owner.

Suitable for	Higher rate taxpayers and people who want a secure investment.
Open to	Anyone.
Min–Max	Around £2,000; no maximum.
Charges	None. The market maker (who buys and sells the policies) takes a turn on the transaction. Policy charges built into the contract.
Withdrawals	The policy can be surrendered early but there will still be a penalty.

Interest	Variable; built into bonuses.
Tax	Returns are net of all taxes except capital gains tax.
Children	Yes.
How to invest	The Association of Policy Market Makers (0171-739 3949) will provide a list of companies which deal in second-hand endowment policies. It is also possible to buy them at auction. Foster & Cranfield (0171-608 1941) specialises in such auctions.
Record	Assigned policy.
Money Mail rating	****!
Investor protection	Market makers belong to PIA.
Comment	Second-hand policies offer the relatively secure investment of a with-profits policy at a cheaper cost than buying one from scratch. Good when planning for specific financial outlays. It is now possible to buy investment trusts which specialise in second-hand policies.

Unit-Linked Regular Savings Plan

A regular savings insurance policy for five or 10 years or indefinitely, linked directly to an individual market sector, or to a mixture of different types of investment. Savings can be linked to specific unit trusts, UK equities, international equities, fixed interest stock, cash, property or a mixture of some or all of these categories. Investors can switch their savings from one category to another.

Suitable for	One-stop financial planning, as policies can be adapted to provide more protection and less investment content, and vice-versa at different intervals, such as marriage or the birth of children; insurance backing to a mortgage instead of a conventional endowment policy.

LIFE INSURANCE

Open to	Varies; anyone from 13 to 70 years old.
Min–Max	£10–£50 minimum; no maximum.
Charges	Policy fee – from none to £1.30 per month; the initial fee of 4–5 per cent is deducted from the premium; annual fee ¾–1 per cent.
Withdrawals	After 10 years you get the value of the units; before that there might be a capital gains tax liability. There is usually surrender penalty if the policy encashed in early years.
Interest	Variable; accumulated within the fund.
Tax	Income tax and capital gains tax on both the realised and unrealised gains paid by the insurance company, reflected in the underlying unit price. Proceeds are tax free after 10 years; on earlier encashment, higher rate taxpayers pay more.
Children	Yes, where age limits permit.
How to invest	Check the performance of underlying units in specialist publications such as *Money Management* or *Planned Savings*; most companies offer this contract, so phone or write for details. Independent intermediaries will be able to advise on these schemes.
Record	Insurance policy and annual unit valuation.
Money Mail Rating	****! to *!!!!
Investor protection	Policyholders' protection scheme covers 90 per cent of current unit value.
Comment	The capital gains tax liability on underlying investments is a major disadvantage compared with regular savings directly into unit trusts which roll up free of capital gains tax. As the proceeds are tax free, however, there can be tax planning opportunities. These unit-linked plans are becoming increasingly

popular as an alternative to endowment policies for backing an interest-only mortgage. If the underlying units rise rapidly, the home loan can be repaid earlier.

With-Profits Endowment Policy

A regular savings policy for a fixed period of 10 years or more. A guaranteed sum assured is paid out on death before the end of the set term or at maturity *plus* any bonuses which the policy has earned from the underlying investments. There are two kinds of bonuses: those declared annually ("reversionary bonuses", which can never be taken away from the policy), and a "terminal bonus", which can vary, paid out at maturity.

Suitable for	Nowadays used mainly in connection with house purchase, particularly the "low cost" endowment variation; regular savings which are not required for several years.
Open to	Anyone from eight years old.
Charges	Built into the contract; policy fee of around £1 a month.
Min–Max	£5–£10 a month minimum; no maximum.
Withdrawals	On maturity or the death beforehand of the life assured (usually the policyholder's, but it can be another person in whom you have an "insurable", in other words financial, interest). Surrender values are non-existent or very low in the first few years, and the surrender penalty remains heavy for several or many years afterwards. Alternatively, the policyholder can stop paying premiums and make the policy "paid up" at a reduced benefit level. It is also possible to take out a loan against the policy from the insurance company, often at competitive rates.
Interest	Variable; built into bonuses.

LIFE INSURANCE

Tax	Income tax and capital gains tax on realised profits paid by the insurance company, reflected in the level of bonuses. Policy proceeds after 10 years are completely tax free, but on earlier encashment higher rate taxpayers can pay more.
Children	Policies "in trust" for a child avoid inheritance tax; children over eight years can take out a policy, but a parent's signature is required up to 18.
How to invest	Consult an independent financial adviser or obtain quotes direct from life offices and compare. Equitable Life, which does not pay commission, will not be included on broker quotations.
Record	Insurance policy; annual bonus statement.
Money Mail Rating	****!
Investor protection	Policyholders' protection scheme covers 90 per cent of benefits.
Comment	Long-term endowment policies with harsh surrender policies should be avoided. This is an inflexible and increasingly outmoded form of savings, largely used now in connection with house purchase. Terminal bonus rates have begun to be lower in the last two years.

With-Profits Flexible Policy

A regular savings policy for an indefinite period, which should be for at least 10 years. On death a guaranteed sum assured is paid out plus any bonuses which the policy has earned from its underlying investments. After 10 years the policy can be encashed at any time without a surrender penalty at a guaranteed or part-guaranteed value. The policy is often issued as a cluster of small identical policies which can each be cashed in separately.

Suitable for	Regular savings, particularly for specific targets, such as school fees, needed at least 10 years hence.

LIFE INSURANCE

Open to	Anyone from eight years.
Min–Max	£10–£25 a month minimum; no maximum.
Charges	Built into the contract; policy fee of around £1 a month.
Withdrawals	On the death of the life assured, when a guaranteed sum assured plus bonuses is paid; at guaranteed surrender value any time after 10 years. Harsh surrender penalties apply to withdrawals before 10 years.
Interest	Variable; built into bonuses.
Tax	Income tax and capital gains tax on the realised profits paid by the insurance company, reflected in the level of bonuses. Policy proceeds after 10 years are completely tax free, but on earlier encashment higher rate taxpayers can pay more.
Children	Policies "in trust" for a child avoid inheritance tax; children over eight years can take out a policy, but a parent's signature required up to 18.
How to invest	Consult an insurance broker or obtain quotes direct from life offices and compare.
Record	Insurance policy; annual bonus statement.
Money Mail Rating	****!
Investor protection	Policyholders' protection scheme covers 90 per cent of benefits.
Comment	More flexible than a with-profit endowment policy which it was partially designed to replace. Cluster policies, where each bit can be cashed separately, give more flexibility still. At maturity proceeds can be left intact and a nominal premium, around £5 p.a., allows the policyholder to withdraw regular tax-free "income" from the policy, or take out tax-free money at irregular intervals.

LIFE INSURANCE

With-Profit Bonds

Broadly the same as a with-profits endowment policy but for a lump sum investment rather than regular savings. Effectively an investment in the equity and property markets, usually with an element of gilts and cash, but the fluctuations are smoothed out by the insurance companies who use their reserves to bolster the return in poor years, replenishing those reserves in good years. The bond earns a return through two types of bonus: those declared annually ("reversionary bonuses", which can never be taken away from the policy), and a "terminal bonus", which can vary, paid out at maturity.

Suitable for	Investors who want to "strip out" an income and for those who want to benefit from stockmarket/property growth without the usual fluctuations.
Open to	Anyone.
Charges	Built into the contract.
Min–Max	£1,000–£5,000; no maximum.
Withdrawals	On demand at current market value, but the company can use a market value adjuster to reduce the value if market conditions are exceptionally poor. On death at current market value of units.
Charges	Initial fee usually of around 5 per cent but can be reduced for larger investments. An annual fee is built into the contract.
Interest	None, but withdrawals can be made on a regular basis by selling units monthly, quarterly, half-yearly or annually. This can provide an income at whatever level the investor chooses.
Tax	Income tax and capital gains tax on realised profits paid by insurance company, reflected in level of bonuses. Policy proceeds are tax free but higher rate taxpayers can pay more.

LIFE INSURANCE

Children	Policies "in trust" for a child avoid inheritance tax if held for seven years and could mitigate inheritance tax if held for shorter periods. Children over eight can invest but a parent's signature is required until 18.
How to invest	Consult a financial adviser or obtain quotes direct from life offices and compare. Look for companies with a good record of bonus payments and good reserves.
Record	Insurance policy; annual bonus statement.
Money Mail Rating	****!
Investor protection	Policyholders' protection scheme covers 90 per cent of benefits.
Comment	Can buy/sell on any business day but should be regarded as a long-term investment if stripping out an income.

Temporary Annuity and "Back to Backs"

A temporary annuity is a lump sum investment which cannot be redeemed, in return for a high income for a specified period, usually five or 10 years. There is no return of capital at maturity so it is common to link the temporary annuity with a growth vehicle – usually an investment bond, unit trust or PEP – which is designed to return the original capital. This is called a "back-to-back" arrangement. A £10,000 investment can, for example, be split into a £4,000 temporary annuity to provide a high income over five years and a £6,000 PEP investment which it is hoped will grow to £10,000 over the five years.

Suitable for	Anyone looking for a high regular income who is prepared to accept the moderate degree of risk.
Open to	Anyone.

LIFE INSURANCE

Min–Max	Usually £5,000; no maximum.
Charges	Built into the contract. See appropriate sections for growth vehicles.
Interest	Fixed. Usually paid in arrears by cheque or direct to a bank account monthly, quarterly, half-yearly or annually.
Tax	Part of the annuity is treated as a return of capital and is tax free, the remainder is treated as income and is paid net of basic rate tax. Non-taxpayers can be paid gross; higher rate taxpayers pay more. See appropriate sections for growth vehicles.
Children	Possible but not particularly suitable.
How to invest	Look for advertisements in the financial press and check performances of growth vehicles in specialist publications such as *Money Management* or *Planned Savings*; phone or write to the relevant companies to ask for details before investing.
Record	Annuity contract.
Money Mail Rating	*****
Investor protection	Policyholders' protection scheme covers 90 per cent of annuity benefits.
Comment	Usually a way of providing a better income than a building society, but much depends on the performance of the growth vehicle. It could provide a return equal to or more than the original capital but there is a risk that it could provide less. See comment in appropriate sections for each type of growth vehicle.

CHAPTER 15

Local Authorities

Local Authority Bond

A lump sum investment in the form of a fixed term loan to a local authority which pays a fixed rate of interest for a set period of one to 10 years. Shorter term loans are available for larger sums.

Suitable for	Lock-away savings only or savings with a specific target date; five years is generally long enough to commit yourself to one form of savings. Non-taxpayers should consider Government stock on the National Savings Stock Register.
Open to	Anyone aged 18 or over.
Min–Max	Varies. Minimum can be as little as £200–£500, although £1,000 is more common.
Charges	None.
Withdrawals	Not permitted until end of term.
Interest	Fixed; usually paid half-yearly. But rates vary sharply from local authority to local authority.
Tax	Interest paid net of 20 per cent tax; 40 per cent higher rate taxpayers pay the difference of 20 per cent tax extra. Local authorities can pay interest gross to non-taxpayers.

LOCAL AUTHORITIES

Children	An investment can be made on behalf of a child, but this is not really suitable.
How to invest	Newspaper coupons, or direct from a local authority (treasurer's department).
Record	Certificate.
Money Mail Rating	*****
Comment	When interest rates are falling, fixed rate returns can be attractive (conversely if they are rising). The main drawback is the inflexibility. The fixed term means precisely what it says: most local authority treasurers will not permit early repayment, no matter the hardship: death is the only exception. Investors with more than £25,000 might be able to negotiate better rates.

Negotiable or Yearling Bond

A lump sum investment paying a fixed rate of interest for a set period, normally one year, hence the name "yearling". Local authorities parcel up a selection of loan requirements into a single bond which can be bought and sold on the Stock Exchange. Investors don't identify the specific authorities behind the issue but treat it like any other fixed interest, negotiable security, such as Government stock. The bonds might be issued at a very small discount to the nominal value.

Suitable for	Any short-term fixed interest investment where flexibility is required.
Open to	Anyone aged 18 or over.
Min–Max	Buy in multiples of £1,000, the minimum investment is £1,000. No maximum.
Charges	None, if bought as a new issue from a stockbroker and held to redemption; otherwise stockbroker's commission if you buy and sell between those dates.

LOCAL AUTHORITIES

Withdrawals — Hold to maturity for return of full nominal value or sell before on the Stock Exchange where the price can vary.

Interest — Fixed, paid half-yearly; any interest due is added to the selling price if you sell the bonds early.

Tax — Tax is deducted at source at 20 per cent but can be reclaimed by non-taxpayers; 40 per cent higher rate taxpayers pay the difference of 20 per cent tax extra. If you sell at a profit the gain is liable to capital gains tax.

Children — Investment can be made on behalf of a child, but is not suitable.

How to invest — Through a stockbroker or bank share dealing service.

Record — Certificate.

Money Mail Rating — If held to maturity *****. If sold early ****!

Comment — Flexible: if there is any upward movement in interest rates you are not locked in; if rates fall you can stay put at the bond's higher fixed rate. Compare rates with those on Government stock.

CHAPTER 16

National Savings

FIRST Option Bond

Traditionally National Savings schemes have been directed at non-taxpayers, but this saving plan is a guaranteed investment bond, with the tax deducted at source. FIRST actually stands for Fixed Interest Rate Savings Tax-Paid. The rate is guaranteed for a year, when savers have the option of either continuing with the investment for another 12 months, at the then guaranteed interest rate, or encashing the bond.

Suitable for	Taxpayers, although non-taxpayers will be able to reclaim the tax paid on the interest. Poor return for higher rate taxpayers.
Open to	Anyone over the age of 16. Joint holdings are accepted and trustees can hold them for personal beneficiaries.
Min–Max	£1,000–£250,000. There is no "topping up" as each purchase is a separate bond.
Charges	None.
Withdrawals	In whole or in part of any anniversary date; no notice period is required. However, if the bond is cashed before the first anniversary, no interest will be paid. Thereafter withdrawals between anniversaries would attract half interest for the period from the previous anniversary.

NATIONAL SAVINGS

Interest — Guaranteed at the time of purchase for 12 months, and added to the capital at each anniversary. The current rate is 5.0% net (6.25% gross); an investment of £20,000 plus earns a bonus of 0.2% net (0.25% gross) after 12 months.

Tax — Tax of 20 per cent is deducted at source before the interest is credited to the bond. Non-taxpayers will be eligible for a tax refund. Forty per cent higher rate taxpayers will pay the difference of 20 per cent tax more.

Children — Not until age 16.

How to invest — Direct from National Savings, Glasgow G58 1SB. Forms are available from post offices or ring 0645-645000, local rates apply.

Record — Certificate.

Money Mail Rating — *****

Comment — After the first year, the bond is a relatively flexible addition to the National Savings repertoire. While the Government continues to need to raise funds from National Savings, the interest rate structure should remain quite attractive for basic rate taxpayers. Higher rate taxpayers should look at National Savings tax free products first.

Capital Bond

Series "J"

A lump sum investment with a low minimum required. It is similar in format to National Savings Certificates but interest is paid gross, and is taxable in the hands of basic and higher rate taxpayers. Interest, which is accumulated, is calculated daily and added on to the bond annually. Designed as a five year investment. Tax, however, has to be paid annually.

Suitable for — Non-taxpayers, children's savings and basic rate taxpayers who can leave their savings locked up for five years.

NATIONAL SAVINGS

Open to Anyone.

Min–Max £100–£250,000 (including total holdings in Capital Bonds since Series "B").

Charges None.

Withdrawals In full, or partial withdrawals in multiples of £100 providing a balance of £100 retained.

Interest Calculated daily, accumulated before tax annually and fixed at set rates for five year term. At the end of year one: 4.6 per cent, year two: 5.2 per cent, year three: 6.1 per cent, year four: 7.7 per cent, year five: 9.7 per cent (all gross rates) giving gross compound interest rate of 6.65 per cent a year. The net return to basic rate taxpayers is 5.32 per cent, after tax of 20 per cent.

Tax Interest is accumulated gross, and has to be declared on your tax return each year although payment won't be received until the bonds are encashed. Basic rate taxpayers will pay 20 per cent, higher rate taxpayers, 40 per cent.

Children Yes. Withdrawals to parents or designated trustees can be made on their behalf if under age seven and bonds have matured.

How to invest Application forms are available at any post office or direct from National Savings, Glasgow G58 1SB. Tel: 0645–645000, local rates apply.

Record Certificate.

Money Mail Rating *****

Comment Definitely for savers who can last the five year course. This issue is more attractive than its predecessor. The guaranteed return will look attractive when interest rates begin to fall.

NATIONAL SAVINGS

Children's Bonus Bond
Issue "H"

A new lump sum savings for children under 16 years (who can hold them until age 21). It is a fixed rate, tax-free investment with a return of 6.75 per cent, turning £100 into £138.64, provided the bond is held for the full five years. It is important to keep the bond for five years. Interest is added at the rate of only 5 per cent a year; the real kick comes from the 11 per cent final bonus.

Suitable for	Children under 16 (at time of investment).
Open to	Children under 16.
Min–Max	£25–£1,000.
Charges	None.
Withdrawals	Minimum £25. One month's notice is required for early repayments. No interest is encashed within the first year. Repayment at fifth anniversary (allow 8 days notice) on holder's 21st birthday.
Interest	Fixed; 5 per cent a year plus final bonus of 11 per cent, making a compound annual return of 6.75 per cent if held for the full five years.
Tax	Tax free.
Children	Yes.
How to invest	Application form at post offices. By anyone over the age of 16 on behalf of an individual under 16.
Record	Certificate.
Money Mail Rating	*****

| Comment | A very attractive return. A must for generous grandparents or relatives. But keep the bond for five years to get the maximum benefit. Suitable as a gift from a parent, as the tax-free interest does not (if it exceeds £100) have to be aggregated with the parent's income for tax purposes. |

Deposit Bond

(Withdrawn from sale on 19 November 1988)

A lump sum investment. Interest accumulates. There are surrender penalties on early encashment. Terms and conditions are guaranteed for 10 years.

Charges	None.
Withdrawals	In multiples of £50, provided £100 remains, subject to three months' notice. Interest payable is reduced to half if the bond is encashed in the first 12 months. Repayment forms and post-paid envelopes are available on request at post offices. Payment is by warrant, treat as a cheque.
Interest	Variable, at six weeks' notice; calculated daily, credited on anniversary of purchase. Current rate: 6.25 per cent.
Tax	Not deducted, but interest is taxable and should be declared on tax return. Basic rate taxpayers will pay tax at 20 per cent on the interest; higher rate at 40 per cent.
Money Mail Rating	*****
Comment	Deposit Bonds have, at the most, 2½ years left to run. Consider switching into higher paying building society term shares or guaranteed income bonds. Anyone over age 65 should consider Pensioners Guaranteed Income Bonds as an alternative.

NATIONAL SAVINGS

Income Bond

A lump sum investment paying interest without deduction of tax at source. Interest is variable and usually competitive; it changes less frequently than bank interest rates. There are surrender penalties on early encashment.

Suitable for	Retired people and others needing a steady flow of income who do not need immediate access to their capital. Non-taxpayers in particular benefit from the gross interest payment and the convenience of monthly income.
Open to	Anyone.
Min–Max	Buy in multiples of £1,000; the minimum investment is £2,000, the maximum £250,000.
Charges	None.
Withdrawals	In multiples of £1,000, provided £2,000 remains invested, subject to three months' notice. Interest is reduced to half if a bond is encashed within the first 12 months. Alternatively repayment can be made without notice but there will be a penalty of 90 days interest. Repayment forms and pre-paid envelopes are available on request at post offices.
Interest	Variable, at six weeks' notice; paid on the 5th of the month direct to a bank, building society or National Savings Bank, or by crossed warrant (treat as a cheque). The first interest payment is made after the bond has been held for six weeks and includes all interest due from date of investment. Rate: 6.25 per cent gross. Rate for investments of £25,000 or more, 6.5 per cent gross.
Tax	Not deducted, but interest is taxable and should be declared on your tax return. Twenty per cent and basic rate taxpayers will pay tax of 20 per cent; higher rate taxpayers 40 per cent on the interest.
Children	Yes; but not suitable.
How to invest	Application forms available at post offices or by post from National Savings, Blackpool FY3 9YP, or by telephone: 0645–645000, calls at local rates.

NATIONAL SAVINGS

Record	Certificate.
Money Mail Rating	*****
Comment	Gross monthly income is attractive, but if you are a taxpayer the tax will have to be paid. Pensioners Guaranteed Income Bond (see p 110) is much more suitable for anyone aged 65 or over. Although interest is variable it is not likely to rise substantially (it can also fall): some investment providing rising income is also desirable.

Investment Account

A National Savings Bank account using post office counters paying a competitive interest rate, although it changes less frequently than other banks' interest rate. Interest, which does not have tax deducted at source, accumulates.

Suitable for	Non-taxpayers including children who do not require immediate access to their funds; for irregular savings of different amounts.
Open to	Anyone.
Min–Max	Any amount of £20 or more for each deposit. Maximum investment of £100,000 does not include interest credited to the account.
Charges	None.
Withdrawals	One month's notice from the date your application is received at National Savings Bank HQ paid by crossed warrant (treat as a cheque) or cash at a named post office. Alternatively money can be withdrawn immediately with 30 days loss of interest. Repayment forms and pre-paid envelopes are available on request at post offices.
Interest	Variable; automatically credited to accounts on 31 December. Bank books should be sent to National Savings Bank, Glasgow G58 1SB, to have interest entered. Annual interest statement is available on

NATIONAL SAVINGS

request. Current rate up to £500: 5.0 per cent; £500+: 5.5 per cent; £25,000+: 5.75 per cent gross.

Tax Not deducted, but interest is taxable and should be declared on your tax return. The National Savings Bank has to inform the Inland Revenue of interest paid on each account. Basic rate taxpayers will pay tax at 20 per cent; higher rate taxpayers at 40 per cent.

Children Yes, but no withdrawals for under-sevens. Investment can be made by parents as trustee when the same conditions apply; withdrawals after seven will require the child's signature as well. Relatives or friends can open an account in a child's name; no withdrawals under the age of seven, afterwards the child can withdraw on own signature.

How to invest Application form at post offices; fill in a form at the post office for subsequent deposits or apply direct to National Savings Bank, Glasgow G58 1SB, or ring free 0800–100 100. Dividends from shares and Government stock can be credited directly to the account.

Record Bank book.

Money Mail Rating *****

Comment Not a substitute for a high-interest cheque book account; judge on investment rather than banking merits. Gross interest payments are attractive. The moderately complicated withdrawal procedure prevents casual usage, for example, by children for whom the account is particularly suitable. It takes longer to get interest credited in January than at any other time of the year, and there is nothing to be gained by sending the bank book off so early.

Ordinary Account

A two-tiered bank account using post office counters offering modest interest, partly tax free, easy access to funds and some banking services.

NATIONAL SAVINGS

Suitable for — Day-to-day money management of people who either have no bank current account or are frequent users of the post office, for example to draw a pension or other benefits. Higher rate taxpayers who benefit from the partly tax-free interest.

Open to — Anyone.

Min–Max — £10–£10,000.

Charges — None.

Withdrawals — Up to £100 on demand at any post office. "Regular Customer Account" permits up to £250 in cash a day at one chosen post office where you have been a customer for a least six months. Written applications are required for larger withdrawals; forms and pre-paid envelopes are available on request at post offices.

Bills normally paid at the post office e.g., TV licence, road tax – totalling not more than £250 at a time can be paid directly from the account.

Interest — Provided the account is open for the full calendar year, investors earn a guaranteed 2.75 per cent for each calendar month that there is £500 or more in the account, otherwise 1.75 per cent. No interest is payable on the month in which the investment or withdrawal is made.

Tax — Not deducted at source and as partly taxable it should be declared, in full, on your tax return. The first £70 of interest is tax free (capital required £1,400). After that basic rate taxpayers pay tax at 20 per cent, higher rate taxpayers at 40 per cent.

Children — Yes, but no withdrawals for under-sevens; relatives or friends can open an account in a child's name but no withdrawals under seven; afterwards a child can withdraw on own signature.

How to invest — Application form at post offices; fill in a form at the post office for subsequent deposits.

Record — Bank book.

NATIONAL SAVINGS

Money Mail Rating *****

Comment Alternative to bank current account for people who want instant record of transactions. If you cannot keep £500 in the account, a building society ordinary account will pay more even if interest is paid net of tax; with £500 or more, a building society cheque or cash card account will usually pay more and offer some banking services too. Interest rates are so low that higher rate taxpayers no longer benefit from keeping their maximum £1,400 (for tax-free interest).

9th Issue Index-Linked Certificates

A lump sum investment, popularly known as "Granny Bonds" (before the new Pensioners Guaranteed Income Bond was launched in 1994), for small to medium-sized amounts which will both grow in line with increases in the cost of living, as measured by the Retail Prices Index, and earn guaranteed interest each year. Certificates have to be held for 12 months to qualify for index-linking. The repayment value of certificates is published each month in the press and listed in post offices. This latest issue has a low scale of annual bonuses, although the final compound bonus is attractive.

Suitable for Most investors when the rate of inflation looks set to increase, but more suitable for higher rate taxpayers than non-taxpayers.

Open to Anyone.

Min–Max Minimum of £100, bought in units of £25; maximum £10,000 (400 units). This is in addition to any other holdings, index-linked and conventional, of National Savings Certificates. A further £20,000 from matured issues of other certificates (index-linked or conventional) and Yearly Plan can be invested in this issue.

Charges None.

Withdrawals — Eight working days' notice is required. Repayment form and pre-paid envelope are available at post offices. Partial withdrawals are permitted. If withdrawn in first year, money back only without interest.

Interest — Guaranteed for five years. Index-linking is added at the end of the first year on the anniversary of purchase and thereafter the value of certificates moves in line with changes in the Retail Price Index. Extra, guaranteed interest is added.

At the end of year one, interest of 1.0 per cent of the purchase price is added. At succeeding anniversaries the interest is calculated on the value of the bond (including indexation and earlier interest) twelve months before. For example, interest at the end of year 2 is calculated on the value of the bond at the end of year one. Interest added at year two is 1.25 per cent; 2.0 per cent, year three; 3.0 per cent, year four; and 5.31 per cent at the end of year five. The compound annual interest rate is 2.5 per cent, on top of index-linking, over five years. After year five, index-linking will continue and variable rate interest will be paid.

Tax — Free of income tax and capital gains tax and need not be declared on your tax return.

Children — Yes, but children have to be aged over seven before certificates can be encashed other than in exceptional circumstances, such as great hardship. Certificates held in trust do not count towards the individual's own maximum investment.

How to invest — Most post offices and banks have application forms. Quote your holder's number if you have one.

Record — Certificate. A holder's card which has registered number under which all certificates are held is issued at first purchase of any certificate. This number is quoted on all certificates of whatever issue is bought.

Money Mail Rating — *****

Investor protection — Guaranteed by Government.

Comment	Higher rate taxpayers should top up their holding of tax-free certificates. Provided certificates are held for 12 months, a fairly flexible form of savings.

43rd Issue Savings Certificates

A lump sum investment for modest amounts which should be held for five years to obtain the maximum benefits, which are tax free, although earlier withdrawals are possible.

Suitable for	Long-term savings, gifts to children. Particularly attractive to higher rate taxpayers: non-taxpayers should avoid.
Open to	Anyone.
Min–Max	£100 (four units); maximum £10,000, but savers of matured issues of savings certificates, including index-linked certificates, can reinvest up to £20,000 of the proceeds in this issue.
Charges	None.
Withdrawals	Any number of units. Repayment forms and pre-paid envelopes are available at post offices; allow two weeks for repayment either by warrant (treated as a cheque) or cash at the post office.
Interest	If held for the full five years, the compound annual rate of interest works out at 5.35 per cent a year. No interest is paid until the end of the first year, thereafter it is paid at three-monthly intervals. At the end of year one, 3.75 per cent is added; 4.15 per cent at the end of year two; 5.0 per cent year three; 6.15 per cent year four; and 7.75 per cent at the end of year five. Investors cashing in "reinvested certificates" in the first year will receive interest, at the rate of 3.75 per cent a year, for each complete three-month period.
Tax	The interest is tax free and need not be declared on your tax return.

NATIONAL SAVINGS

Children	Suitable for gifts to children; certificates in a child's name cannot be encashed until the child is seven.
How to invest	At your local post office. If it is a second or subsequent purchase of certificates (any issue), you will need your holder's number card.
Record	Certificate. If it is your first purchase of certificates you will be given a holder's number card which covers all future purchases of certificates you might make. Quote this number for subsequent purchases or any withdrawals.
Money Mail rating	*****
Investor protection	Guaranteed by the Government.
Comment	Higher rate taxpayers should keep their National Savings Certificates topped up. If you think interest rates are going to fall, exercise the option to convert matured holdings into the 41st Issue. Theoretically, if you think interest rates will rise in the next five years, then the variable General Extension Rate interest earned on mature issues offers more flexibility for switching. In practice, the rate is so low (3.51 per cent) it is not worth keeping any money at this rate.

Pensioners Guaranteed Income Bond

Series "3"

A lump sum investment for pensioners paying monthly interest without deduction of tax at source. Interest is fixed for five years.

Suitable for	Retired people who want a fixed level of monthly income and do not need access to their capital.
Open to	Those aged 60 and over only.
Min–Max	£500–£50,000 (£100,000 for joint holdings).

NATIONAL SAVINGS

Charges	None.
Withdrawals	Minimum repayment is £500 and £500 must remain invested. 60 days notice and no interest is paid during the notice period if you want your money back before the end of five years. Alternatively money can be withdrawn immediately with 90 days loss of interest.
Interest	Fixed at 7.0 per cent for five years, paid monthly.
Tax	Not deducted, but interest is taxable so should be declared on your tax form. Basic rate taxpayers will pay tax at 20 per cent on the interest, higher rate taxpayers, 40 per cent.
How to invest	Application forms available at post offices or by post from National Savings, Blackpool FY3 9YP, or by telephone 0645–645000, calls at local rate.
Money Mail	*****
Investor protection	Guaranteed by the Government.
Comment	This is a well designed product for the pensioner. Non-taxpayers don't have to bother about reclaiming tax; taxpayers have the immediate benefit of income paid gross, although have to pay the tax due later. It is a relatively new savings and so far the interest rate has remained quite good.

Premium Bond

In effect, a money-back lottery ticket which has gained in popularity since the launch of the National Lottery. About £4,700 million is invested in Premium Bonds. Once a month ERNIE (Electronic Random Number Indicator Equipment) picks out at random over 190,000 £1 bond numbers which will win prizes ranging from £50 to a "jackpot" of £1 million. Every prize winner is notified by post; the post office lists all the winning numbers and big prize numbers are published in the press. The total number of prizes is now limited to 350,000 which will increase the number of higher value prizes each month.

Suitable for	Anyone wanting a flutter without losing his or her stake money. Tax-free winnings, if any, are attractive for higher rate taxpayers. An alternative to cash gifts.

NATIONAL SAVINGS

Open to	Anyone.
Min–Max	£1 bonds sold in multiples of £10, minimum investment £100; maximum £20,000. Bonds have to be held for one clear calendar month before being eligible for the draw. Winners of £50 Premium Bond prizes are able to reinvest their prize warrants despite the £100 minimum transaction.
Charges	None.
Withdrawals	Money back only. Partial withdrawals in £10 multiples are allowed. Repayment forms and pre-paid envelopes are available at post offices. Allow eight working days before repayment either by crossed warrant (treated as a cheque) or cash at post offices.
Interest	None. The prize fund is currently calculated at 4.75 per cent of total money invested in Premium Bonds.
Tax	Prizes are free of income tax and capital gains tax and need not be declared on your tax return.
Children	Under the age of 16 bonds must be bought by a parent, guardian or grandparent to whom any prize money will be paid.
Record	Bond which is issued with individual holder's numbers.
Money Mail Rating	*****
Investor protection	Guaranteed by the Government.
Comment	The odds on winning any prize are 11,000 to 1 – and there are many more £50–£100 prizes than there are big ones. A single bond in the minimum multiple of £10 has as much chance of winning as one from a block of £10,000. There are 240,000 unclaimed prizes worth over £13 million at March 1996. Are any of them yours? Holders of the maximum number of bonds tend to obtain a return in line with the prize fund level of 4.75 per cent a year.

NATIONAL SAVINGS

Save As You Earn (SAYE)

4th Issue Series "F" Share Option Scheme

(Withdrawn in November 1994 Budget)

A regular monthly savings linked to a company share option scheme. Employees are offered the option to buy shares at a price fixed at the start of the five year savings period which cannot be less than 80 per cent of their current market value. Employees invest a set amount each month in the SAYE scheme. At the end of five years they can either use the money to exercise the share option or take the money with a bonus. They can leave the money invested for another two years to obtain a higher bonus BUT they will then lose the share option entitlement. However, some employers offer a seven year share option plan when the share option can then be exercised.

Interest in the SAYE accumulates tax free. In addition there is a bonus of 9 months' payments tax free at the end of five years, or 18 months' if you leave the savings in for the next two years. Existing savers can continue in scheme.

Withdrawals	No partial withdrawals. Reduced interest rate penalties on early withdrawal; no interest in year one; years two to five, 5 per cent. If you die, your executor can either take the amount saved or buy shares at the option price.
Interest	Fixed. Including the bonus is equivalent to 5.53 per cent over five years; including the enlarged bonus, the rate over seven years is equivalent to 5.87 per cent. It is accumulated.
Tax	Tax free. Once the share option is exercised, dividends are taxable and there is a potential gains tax liability, based on the actual purchase price of the shares, when you sell them.
Record	Certificate.
Money Mail Rating	***** until the share option is exercised.
Investor protection	SAYE is guaranteed by the Government.

NATIONAL SAVINGS

Comment Keep up with the SAYE. It is a useful way of hedging your bets. If the company's shares have risen since you were granted the option, then you exercise the option and buy the share at the lower price fixed when you began saving. You will have a built-in profit. However, if your company has been less successful and the share price is actually lower than the option price, then take the SAYE proceeds as cash.

Yearly Plan

(Withdrawn on 31 January 1995)

A regular savings plan for one year at fixed rate of interest; the plan is then converted into a certificate and if held for a further four years it earns a higher fixed rate of interest. Interest is reinvested and is tax free.

Charges None.

Withdrawals On 14 days' notice; no partial withdrawals are allowed. Repayment forms and pre-paid envelopes are available at post offices. No interest is payable if the plan is encashed within the first 12 months.

Interest Fixed. If held for full five years 5.85 per cent a year. Rates are lower if you encash the plan earlier: 3.75 per cent p.a. if held for less than two years; 4.75 per cent if held for more than two but less than four years. If six or fewer monthly payments are made, the interest rate is 3.0 per cent p.a.

Tax Free of income tax and capital gains tax and need not be declared on your tax return.

Record Certificate.

Money Mail Rating *****

Investor protection Guaranteed by the Government.

Comment The fixed rate can be attractive when interest rates in general are falling. Higher rate taxpayers should stick with their holdings until they mature.

CHAPTER 17

Offshore Savings

Building Society Account

Several building societies now have branches offshore, principally in the Isle of Man or the Channel Islands, which enable them to pay interest gross to UK investors. There is a range of accounts available including Instant Access, Notice and Fixed Rate Accounts Shares. They tend to have higher minimum investments but otherwise are identical to mainland accounts. Interest, however, is paid without deduction of tax. Interest rates have tended to be higher than "on shore" equivalents.

Suitable for	Non-taxpayers including non-working wives who need gross interest to offset against their new personal tax allowance, children and other non-taxpayers. Taxpayers wishing to defer their tax liability on the interest.
Open to	Anyone.
Min–Max	Varies from £1,000 to £5,000. No maximum.
Charges	None.
Withdrawals	Depends on the type of account: instant access on demand; notice accounts, usually three months; term shares, one or more years.

Interest	Variable; paid gross either half-yearly or annually. Often marginally higher than similar "onshore" account.
Tax	Interest is paid without deduction of tax. Basic rate taxpayers will pay tax at 20 per cent on the interest; higher rate taxpayers at 40 per cent.
Children	Yes. A parent's signature is required for under-sevens.
How to invest	Consult your local branch. Most large societies operate offshore accounts for UK residents.
Record	Passbook plus statements.
Money Mail Rating	*****
Investor protection	Societies' offshore operations are outside the scope of the Investors Protection Act, but under the Building Societies Act 1986, societies are legally bound to bail out any subsidiary which gets into trouble.
Comment	These accounts were designed to appeal to non-working wives in the wake of independent taxation. They were set up, in the main, before the 1990 Budget which abolished composite rate tax from April 1991. Now that societies in the UK are able to offer gross interest to non-taxpayers, most investors will probably prefer to stay "onshore", although the offshore rates are often a little higher. Some societies (National and Provincial, Woolwich and Yorkshire) allow you to choose your annual interest payment date either side of 5 April to suit your tax position. Do not confuse these offshore building society accounts with those designed for non-UK residents only which have always been able to offer gross interest to people not liable to UK tax.

OFFSHORE SAVINGS

Currency Fund

Equivalent to a bank deposit account in a foreign currency of your own choice, although the investment method is to buy and sell shares in the fund. It is possible to own shares in a currency fund denominated in any of the major world currencies and other less obvious ones such as the Danish kroner, Singapore dollar or Irish punt, and ECU (European Currency Unit). With the same management group it is possible to switch from one currency to another.

Suitable for Non-taxpayers; investors taking a view on currency values; future holiday funds.

Open to Anyone aged 18 or over.

Min–Max Varies; commonly £1,000. No maximum.

Charges No initial fee; an annual fee of ¾–1¼ per cent.

Withdrawals Up to seven days.

Interest Variable; paid gross half-yearly or annually in either foreign currency or sterling if the fund is a "distributor" fund. Interest is reinvested if the fund is an "accumulation" fund.

Tax With a distributor fund the income is paid gross and UK taxpayers must declare and pay income tax on the distribution. With an accumulation fund, the interest is rolled up in the fund without deduction of tax, but when the UK investor realises his profit he will pay income tax on the entire capital gain (which includes any currency appreciations as well as reinvested income).

Children Not suitable.

How to invest Check investment performance in specialist publications such as *Money Management*. Prices and addresses of management companies are quoted on the Offshore Funds page of the *Financial Times*.

Record Share certificate.

OFFSHORE SAVINGS

Money Mail Rating	**!!! to *!!!!
Investor protection	Regulations have changed from an investor protection point of view. Offshore tax havens such as the Isle of Man, the Channel Islands and Bermuda are now designated territories which means that each has a supervisory system similar to the UK's, including a compensation scheme. Individual funds which are marketed in this country have to be recognised and the management company regulated.
Comment	As managers can obtain a higher interest rate on the large sums (the investors' pooled shareholdings) they have to invest, a single currency fund is an attractive alternative to an individual foreign currency deposit account. "Managed" currency funds are also available where the investment manager chooses a basket of currencies for you, switching between them depending on the relative outlook for each currency.

High Interest Cheque Account

An interest-bearing current account, usually with a minimum starting investment, at a bank or branch of a UK bank in the Channel Islands or Isle of Man. It operates in the same way as a domestic high interest cheque account but with the interest paid gross, not net. Some banks such as Royal Bank of Canada and Sieger & Friedlander offer multi-currency cheque book. Most banks stipulate a minimum cheque withdrawal; direct debits and standing orders may be permitted; no overdraft facilities.

Suitable for	It is a complementary account to a current account; the gross payment of interest may have cash flow attractions to taxpayers, who will pay the tax later.
Open to	Anyone aged 18 or over (20 in Jersey).
Min–Max	£1,000–£2,500. No maximum.
Charges	Limited number of free cheques at most banks, subsequent ones commonly cost 50p each.

Withdrawals	With a few exceptions, minimum cheque withdrawal of £200–£250.
Interest	Variable, paid into the account quarterly, half-yearly or annually without deduction of tax.
Tax	UK investors declare and pay income tax on the interest. Basic rate taxpayers will pay 20 per cent; higher rate taxpayers at 40 per cent.
Children	Not unless the account is held in an adult's name.
How to invest	Obtain the address of an offshore subsidiary from your local branch of Bank of Scotland, Barclays, Cater Allen, Lloyds, Midland, National Westminster and TSB.
Record	Bank statements.
Money Mail Rating	*****
Investor protection	No deposit protection scheme, so it is essential to choose a bank which is a subsidiary of a UK bank or well known internationally.
Comment	Consider it as an alternative to a domestic high interest current account or instant access building society account.

Managed Currency Fund

A lump sum investment through the purchase of shares in a professionally managed fund based outside the UK which invests in a range of cash deposits and other monetary investments (called "instruments") such as bills, in a variety of foreign currencies. It effectively operates like a unit trust with the hoped-for gain coming not from appreciation in share prices, but from one currency rising in value against another.

Suitable for	Investors who want to hold assets abroad, but do not want to select which currency to hold their money in; non-taxpayers, but there are only marginal tax advantages for UK taxpayers.

Open to	Anyone aged 18 or over.
Min–Max	Usually £1,000; no maximum.
Charges	Initial fee of 3–4 per cent; annual fee of ¾–1¼ per cent.
Withdrawals	Up to seven days.
Interest	Variable, paid either half-yearly or annually if the fund has "distributor" status; or accumulated in an accumulation fund. In both cases interest is paid without deduction of tax at source, but the tax treatment differs.
Tax	Offshore currency funds are either "distributor" funds or "accumulation" funds. With a distributor fund, the income is paid out gross and UK taxpayers declare and pay income tax on the distribution. With an accumulation fund, the interest is rolled up in the fund without deduction of tax, but when the UK investor realises his profit he will pay income tax on the entire capital gain (which includes any currency appreciation as well as reinvested income) he has made.
Children	Must be held on behalf of a child in an adult's name.
How to invest	Consult specialist publications such as *Money Management* for performance records and companies' addresses. Prices and addresses are also listed on the Offshore Funds page of the *Financial Times*.
Record	Share certificate.
Money Mail Rating	**!!! to *!!!!
Investor protection	Regulations have changed from an investor protection point of view. Offshore tax havens such as the Isle of Man, the Channel Islands and Bermuda are now designated territories which means that each has a supervisory system similar to the UK's,

including a compensation scheme. Individual funds which are marketed in this country have to be recognised and the management company regulated.

Comment Check whether the fund has "distributor" status or not. Among UK banks and unit trust management companies with offshore funds are Guinness Flight, Hill Samuel, INVESCO, Old Court (a Rothschild company), Prudential, N. M. Schroder and TSB.

Fixed Rate Term Account

A lump sum, fixed term, fixed interest rate investment with money tied up for one to five years, in a bank, building society or deposit taker in the Channel Islands or Isle of Man. Interest is paid without deduction of tax.

Suitable for Anyone taking a view that interest rates elsewhere will fall.

Open to Anyone.

Min–Max £1,000–£5,000 minimum.

Charges None.

Withdrawals At end of term, other than in exceptional circumstances. There is usually an interest rate penalty for early withdrawal.

Interest Fixed; paid without deduction of tax. Higher rates are sometimes negotiable for larger sums up to £100,000. For shorter term investments interest is payable at maturity, otherwise half-yearly or annually.

Tax UK investors declare and pay income tax on the interest. Basic rate taxpayers will pay tax at 20 per cent; higher rate taxpayers at 40 per cent.

Children Not suitable.

How to invest Obtain addresses of offshore subsidiaries from UK banks.

OFFSHORE SAVINGS

Record	Statement.
Money Mail Rating	*****
Investor protection	No compensation scheme, so it is essential to choose a bank which is a subsidiary of UK bank or deposit taker.
Comment	Short-term cash flow attractions for taxpayers who defer the tax liability. Compare the gross equivalent interest rates of the fixed interest investments where interest has tax deducted at source.

Investment Funds

A lump sum investment in a professionally managed pool of money which is invested in a wide spread of shares, stocks and other assets sometimes known as an OEIC (Open Ended Investment Fund). It is quite similar to a UK authorised unit trust, but has a single price (unlike the bid-offer price of a unit trust). Changes in the law now permit these funds to be sold in the UK, but do not expect to see them until mid-1997.

OEICs will come under the UCITS umbrella. The acronym stands for Undertaking for Collective Investments in Transferable Securities and is the invention of the European Commission to cover all forms of collective investments, such as unit trusts, offered by individual Common Market countries to investors in EU member states. Provided individual investment schemes, such as a unit trust, match the rules of a UCITS, then they can be marketed freely.

Suitable for	Investors wishing to transfer funds outside the UK or to keep foreign-earned assets abroad.
Open to	Anyone.
Min–Max	Varies. Commonly £500–£1,000. No maximum.
Charges	Initial fee of 5–8½ per cent; an annual fee of ½–1 per cent.
Withdrawals	Usually on demand at market price, sometimes at one month's notice.

OFFSHORE SAVINGS

Interest	Variable; paid as a dividend half-yearly without deduction of tax.
Tax	UK investors declare and pay tax on the dividend. Basic rate taxpayers will pay tax at 20 per cent; higher rate taxpayers at 40 per cent. Both are liable to capital gains tax on profits at disposal.
Children	Not suitable.
How to invest	Check specialist publications such *Money Management* for performance records. Prices and addresses of management companies are listed on the Offshore Funds page of the *Financial Times*.
Record	Certificate.
Money Mail Rating	**!!! to !!!!!
Investor protection	When OEICs are sold in the UK they are subject, onshore, to UK investor protection rules. While they are overseas it will always be sensible to stick to investments run by subsidiaries of established UK companies or those which are well known internationally.
Comment	From the pure investment point of view for a UK taxpayer there is little to choose between a UK unit trust and an offshore one. Single pricing is seen as an advantage to many. Much more depends on the motive or need to keep assets offshore.

CHAPTER 18

Pensions

Additional Voluntary Contributions

A tax-free regular savings plan for at least five years, either linked to your company pension scheme or quite separate from it. Your total contributions to your pension scheme and AVC must not exceed 15 per cent of your earnings. All employees who belong to a company pension scheme have the right to make AVC contributions and since October 1987, all employees who belong to a company pension scheme can select their own "free-standing" AVC, outside the firm's pension scheme.

Suitable for	Anyone who began their pension planning late; last minute boost to retirement income; higher rate taxpayers trying to reduce their tax bill.
Open to	Anyone who belongs to an approved company pension scheme.
Min–Max	£5–£10 a month; maximum 15 per cent of your earnings, including mainstream pension scheme contributions on up to a maximum salary of £84,000.
Charges	Built into life assurance schemes; none with building society AVCs.

PENSIONS

Withdrawals — At retirement, as pension and cash commutation with contracts taken out before 17 March 1987; no commutation permitted on AVCs begun since then. If you change jobs, your existing contributions continue to roll up to provide you with a pension based on their value at retirement. If you die before retirement, a full refund plus interest is made.

Tax — Premiums get tax relief in full; the pension is treated as earned income, and the commuted cash sum is tax free.

Children — No.

How to invest — Your pension scheme manager will advise you of the company's own AVC scheme. If choosing your own free stand (FSAVC) scheme, check the performance of the underlying company in the specialist magazines.

Record — Annual statement of contributions, AVC value to date.

Money Mail Rating — Depending on underlying investments ***** to ****!

Investor protection — Policyholders Protection Act covers 90 per cent of benefits promised by UK authorised insurers provided they are not "excessive". Building society investments are covered by the building society compensation scheme.

Comment — The best way of boosting future retirement income. If you have been contributing to your company pension scheme for a long time and can expect a pension of two-thirds of final salary or close to that amount, there will not be any point in paying AVCs as your pension, irrespective of how much you have paid towards it, must not exceed two-thirds of final salary. Your pension scheme manager should alert you to this possibility. If you have "over-funded", new rules permit the excess AVCs to be refunded less tax of 23 per cent.

PENSIONS

Personal Pension Plan

A regular savings scheme for pension provision available from July 1988 which can be bought by employees who do not belong to a company pension scheme; employees who belong to a company pension scheme will also have the option of taking out a personal pension plan instead. Personal pension plans are in effect a refinement of and will have many features in common with Self-Employed Retirement Annuities. The totally new feature is the concessions which will be available to employees taking out a personal pension plan instead of remaining in the State Earnings Related Pension Scheme (SERPS) to which all employees not in a company pension scheme automatically belong. Employers, if they wish, can contribute to your personal pension plan. Building societies and unit trust groups are able to offer personal pensions, as well as insurance companies.

Suitable for Younger, mobile employees, particularly if their company agrees to contribute to the personal pension. The self-employed. House purchase with a pensions mortgage. Older employees who are currently in a company pension scheme are unlikely to benefit.

Open to Self-employed and employees not in a company pension scheme.

Min–Max With a few plans the minimum can be as low as £10 a month (which won't buy you much pension). The maximum is effectively £14,700 (up to age 35), more if older, as contributions are limited to earnings of £84,000. In addition to your contributions, and possibly your employer's, the Government, in some circumstances, will make a contribution too. Employees leaving SERPS to take out a personal pension plan will get the National Insurance rebate for contracting out of SERPS.

Charges Investment in the first one to two years is often in "initial" or "capital" units carrying charges of around 7.5 per cent; thereafter around 0.75 per cent a year.

Withdrawals A pension may be taken from age 50. Cash commutation of 20–25 per cent of individual pension "pot". See Pensions Annuity and Flexible Annuity pages **74** and **76**.

Interest	Variable; reinvested.
Tax	Tax relief in full on contributions of $17\frac{1}{2}$ per cent of earnings up to age 35, 20 per cent of earnings from 36–45, 25 per cent from 46–50, 30 per cent from 51–55, 35 per cent from 56–60 and 40 per cent from 61 years. Pension taxed as income; lump sum tax free.
Children	No.
Record	Policy and statement.
Money Mail Rating	***** to ****!
Investor protection	Personal pension plans come under the investor protection framework of the Financial Services Act: separate arrangements exist for those schemes, such as investments in building society deposits, which are not covered by the Act.
Comment	Employees who are not in a company pension scheme should consider this option carefully. It is rarely if ever appropriate for anyone to transfer out of a company pension scheme with a personal pension plan. You can cease contributions to allow for a career break and restart again. Check the charges. A series of single premiums might be more cost effective than regular premiums for someone planning to take time off.

Self-Employed Retirement Annuity

Regular savings or intermittent lump savings out of tax-free income towards a retirement pension for anyone who does not belong to an occupational pension scheme, a category which includes employees who do not belong to a company pension scheme as well as the self-employed. These contracts ceased to be available from 1 July 1988 when they were replaced by the new Personal Pension Plan (see page **126**), but it is still possible to continue with an existing scheme and make additional contributions to it. Contributions to retirement annuities are invested in insurance-type contract schemes and grow by the addition of bonuses; others resemble unit-linked insurance. At retirement date, the holder has an "open-market" option to choose the highest available annuity, not necessarily the one provided by the company.

Suitable for	Self-employed and those not in a company pension scheme; employees who have an additional source of income not covered by the company pension scheme. House purchase with a pension mortgage. Late pension planning.
Open to	Only to those who took out a plan before 1 July 1988, and who wish to either increase their contributions or carry forward payments for the previous six years.
Min–Max	Regular premiums £10 a month, single premium £500–£1,000. Maximum depends on your earnings and age. It is 17.5 per cent up to age 50, 20 per cent for 51–55, 22.5 per cent for 56–60 and 27.5 per cent for 61 and over.
Charges	Built into the contract for with-profits type schemes; initial fees of 5 per cent and annual ¾ per cent with unit-linked schemes.
Withdrawals	As a pension starting at age 60–75 (the age must be specified at the outset), earlier dates are permitted for special occupations such as money-market brokers and footballers; up to around one-third of the pension fund can be taken as a tax-free cash lump sum but for contracts taken out from 17 March 1987 the sum must not exceed £150,000. See Pension Annuity and Flexible Annuity pages **74** and **76**.
Interest	Variable; reinvested in the pension fund.
Tax	Tax relief in full on the premiums is given to the level appropriate to your age. You can carry forward contributions, and obtain tax relief, for the preceding six years and forward one year. The cash lump sum is tax free; the pension is taxed as earned income.
Children	No.
How to invest	No longer available for new investors.

Record	Pensions policy and statements.
Money Mail Rating	***** to ****!
Investor protection	Policies issued by UK insurance companies are covered by a compensation scheme providing 90 per cent of benefits provided they are not "excessive". Intermediaries selling pensions policies must belong to a self-regulatory organisation.
Comment	Although you cannot start a new Self-Employed Retirement Annuity, you can keep an existing one in force and top it up too. It has two main advantages over personal pension plans: you can take a bigger lump sum out of it – three times the pension after a cash lump has been taken, compared with a maximum of 25 per cent of the pension fund with a personal pension plan; and for policies begun before 1987, the cash lump sum is not restricted to £150,000. However, the amount of tax-free earnings that can be put into a SERA is lower than for Personal Pension Plans (see page **126**).

Transfer Plan

(Or *Section 32 Buy Out Bond*)

All job changers now have the choice of leaving their deferred pension with the ex-employer or taking the transfer value of their pension entitlement either to their new company or to the insurance market to purchase a Transfer Plan, often known as a Buy Out Bond. Some companies might only permit such a transfer in respect of pension rights built up since January 1986, when they were compelled to offer job leavers this choice. The money is invested in an individual account and at retirement age, 60–70, is used to buy either a fixed or rising income pension.

Suitable for	Anyone changing jobs who belongs to an occupational pension scheme, or who is made redundant.
Open to	See above.
Min–Max	In practice £1,000; no maximum.

Charges	Included in the investment.
Withdrawals	At retirement only and as a pension only, apart from a tax-free lump sum cash commutation of up to about one-quarter of your final pension fund.
Interest	Variable, and accumulated within the pension fund.
Tax	Cash sum commuted is tax free, and the pension in payment is taxed as earned income.
Children	No.
How to invest	Consult your outgoing pension scheme manager for details of your pension transfer value. Some companies prefer to handle the arrangements; others will be more amenable to accepting your choice of company for the Buy Out Bond. An insurance broker, or possibly the pension scheme manager at your new job, will also be able to give advice. Most insurance companies market Buy Out Bonds, including Equitable Life, Legal & General, London & Manchester, London Life, NPI, Scottish Widows, Standard Life, Sun Life.
Record	Policy document.
Money Mail Rating	****!
Investor protection	Policyholders' Protection Act covers 90 per cent of insurance benefits provided they are not "excessive". This only applies to authorised UK insurance companies.
Comment	Buy Out Bonds commonly provide a higher pension than a deferred pension with your former employer. In many ways, the Personal Pension Plan can be used as a more flexible alternative. However, you should always take advice before moving your pension arrangements.

If you have a pensions problem, such as a suspected miscalculation of a pension or any other unresolved dispute with your existing or former pension scheme, then the Occupational Pensions Advisory Service can help. It is a charity advised by leading people from the pensions industry, and its services are free to pensioners and employees who have exhausted any discussions with the company pension scheme. It will not advise on any current pensions decision you may be considering – such as to stay with a company pension scheme or opt for a new personal pension plan. Occupational Pensions Advisory Service, 11 Belgrave Road, London SW1V 1RB; Tel: 0171–233 8080. If appropriate it will pass your case to the Pensions Ombudsman scheme which covers all aspects of the pensions industry.

If you suspect you may have been mis-sold a personal pensions policy, tell the PIA Pensions Unit. Tel: 0171–417 7001.

If you have lost contact with a previous employer, or the firm has gone out of business, the Pension Schemes Registry will be able to help you track down any "missing" or "lost" pension. Tel: 0191–225 6393.

There is little doubt that many people were badly advised to switch into personal pensions from a company pension scheme between 1988 and 1994. Most people in this category are having their cases investigated. If you believe you were mis-sold a personal pension in that period, then contact the PIA (Personal Investment Authority) Pensions Unit. Tel: 0171–417 7001.

CHAPTER 19

Shares

Business Expansion Scheme and Fund (Closed December 1993)

These were a lump sum investment in a single company or housing venture. Tax relief was given at the investor's top rate of tax on investments up to £40,000 a year – provided the investment was not realised within five years. So anyone with a BES of under five years should not dispose of it until that crucial anniversary has been passed.

The BES has been replaced by the Enterprise Investment Scheme (see below).

Enterprise Investment Scheme

When the Government announced that it would axe the Business Expansion Scheme at the end of 1993, it soon became apparent that some sort of successor scheme for investors to back small, unquoted companies would be needed. The Enterprise Investment Scheme (EIS) was announced in the first November Budget in 1993, and came into effect in January 1994. Unlike BES, the new Scheme does not extend to investment in housing. Limited tax relief is given to investors provided the shares are held for five years. If the proceeds from other investments are invested in an EIS, any capital gains tax due on the first investment can be deferred.

Open to Anyone except employees or shareholders of the company. However, unlike the BES, an investor can become a paid director of the company provided he or she was not connected with it before the EIS shares were issued.

SHARES

Suitable for — Long-term investors who are happy to accept the risks as well as the potential rewards of backing small companies; they are particularly suited to "hands-on" investors who might wish to get involved in the running of the company. Investors with a substantial capital gains tax liability

Min–Max — The minimum is £500 to £1,000. The maximum is £100,000. It is possible to carry back half of any amount invested between 6 April and 5 October into the previous tax year, up to a maximum of £15,000.

Charges — These vary so check any prospectus carefully.

Withdrawals — At any time, provided you can find a purchaser. If you sell within five years you will lose the tax relief.

Interest — Few companies are expected to pay dividends within the first five years; if they were to, the interest would be taxable.

Tax — You can claim tax relief at 20 per cent only on an EIS. Provided the shares are held for five years, you will not be liable to capital gains tax on their disposal; if you end up with a capital loss, you will be able to offset that against gains. Capital gains tax liability on other investments reinvested in an EIS is deferred.

Children — Not suitable.

How to invest — Information about companies looking for backers should be available from local Training and Enterprise Councils, the Capital Exchange (01568–611555) or the "Business Angels" schemes run by most major banks.

Record — Share certificate.

Money Mail Rating — !!!!!

Investor Protection — If sponsors are used, they must belong to one of the self-regulatory organisations and investors are covered by the appropriate compensation scheme, to a maximum of £48,000.

SHARES

Comment — Not for widows and orphans. EIS is a high risk–high reward investment, most suited to businessmen with capital and maybe time to spare.

Investment Trusts

An investment collective: individual shareholders' funds are pooled and invested in a professionally managed, well-spread portfolio of stocks and shares. Unlike a unit trust, an investment trust is a publicly quoted company whose shares are quoted on the Stock Exchange and rise and fall in value according to demand. Sometimes shares are traded above the "net asset value", the underlying market value of the underlying portfolio of shares, in which case they stand at a "premium"; often they stand at a "discount", that is are traded below the net asset value. Traditionally investment trusts had very general portfolios; nowadays many of them specialise in certain geographical areas, such as Europe or Japan.

Suitable for — Long-term investors; smaller lump sums; investors wanting to concentrate on one specific investment area.

Open to — Anyone.

Min–Max — Theoretically no minimum, but a stockbroker's commission makes investment in amounts below £500 less worthwhile. No maximum.

Charges — Stockbroker's commission. Commission fees are now around 1.85 per cent (less for deals over £7,000–£8,000), and often with a minimum of £20–£25.

Withdrawals — Sell shares in any amount through a stockbroker at current market price. You will receive your money in two to three weeks.

Interest — Variable, called "dividend" and usually paid half-yearly by cheque or direct to your bank account.

Tax — Interest is paid net of 20 per cent tax. The amount deducted, known as the "tax credit", can be reclaimed by non-taxpayers; higher rate taxpayers pay more. Although an investment trust itself is not liable to capital gains tax, gains made by investment trust company shareholders are liable to capital gains tax.

SHARES

Children	Shares bought for a child must be registered in an adult's name.
How to invest	Through a stockbroker or a bank's share-dealing service after asking their advice; consult specialist publications for up-to-date commentary and views on the 200 or so investment trusts available. Unlike unit trusts, investment trusts cannot be sold by off-the-page advertisements.
Record	Share certificate.
Money Mail Rating	***!! to *!!!!
Investor protection	Most management companies to belong to the Investment Management Regulatory Organisation (IMRO) and investors are covered by its compensation scheme, maximum £48,000.
Comment	Investment trusts are more complicated than unit trusts because the share price can move independently of the underlying market value of the portfolio, but in the last 10 years investment trusts, on average, have proved more rewarding than unit trusts.

Investment Trust Savings Scheme

A regular savings scheme for an unlimited period into an investment trust. Monthly contributions are collected and invested at advantageous dealing costs. In addition there is also a dividend reinvestment service (not restricted to the dividend of a specific investment trust) and a facility for making small occasional purchases of investment trust shares either for self or as gift.

Suitable for	Regular modest savings topped up by occasional lump sum investment. A cheaper-than-average way into the stock market.
Open to	Anyone.

SHARES

Min–Max	£20–£25 a month, £250 occasional lump sum. No maximum.
Charges	Trust managers are able to negotiate much lower stockbroker buying charges, usually up to 0.2 per cent, for block purchases of trust shares. 50p per transaction.
Withdrawals	You can sell shares through a stockbroker at current market prices, and, in the majority of cases, at normal stockbroker fees, although managers are increasingly able to offer a special dealing rate on disposals too. You will receive your money in two to three weeks.
Interest	Variable, called "dividend" and usually paid half-yearly either by cheque or direct to your bank account.
Tax	Interest is paid net of 20 per cent rate tax. The amount deducted, known as the "tax credit", can be reclaimed by non-taxpayers; higher rate taxpayers must pay more. Although an investment trust is itself not liable to capital gains tax, gains made by investment trust company shareholders are liable to capital gains tax.
Children	Shares bought for a child must be registered in an adult's name.
How to invest	Apply to an investment trust secretary or manager of a group.
Record	Share certificate.
Money Mail Rating	***!! to *!!!!
Investor protection	Most management companies belong to IMRO, the Investment Management Regulatory Organisation, and investors are covered by its compensation scheme, maximum £48,000.

SHARES

Comment The number of investment trusts and managements seeking to expand their market with savings schemes is growing. Many of AITC's 292 members are included in savings schemes: some of the best known are run by Alliance, Baillie Gifford, Dunedin, Fleming, Foreign & Colonial, Ivory & Sime and Touche Remnant. Twenty groups are now offering an investment trust PEP on a regular savings basis.

Ordinary Quoted

Lump sum investments in shares "quoted" on the Stock Exchange. To achieve that status, the company must have been thoroughly vetted by the Stock Exchange to make sure it is well managed and financially sound; this includes a five-year track record and at least 25 per cent of its share capital sold at the time the company came to the market as a new issue. The investor's objectives are rising dividend income and a rising share price. But shares can fall in value too, and companies have failed.

Suitable for Long-term build-up of capital; short-term speculation. Although the investor hopes to make a profit out of buying shares, remember that it is a risk investment. Shareholders' perks, where available, are a bonus but not a reason for buying.

Open to Anyone.

Min–Max Theoretically, one share in a company can be bought. In practice £400–£500 per shareholding is more realistic, and several shareholdings desirable.

Charges Stockbrokers' fees are no longer fixed. The most common commission for deals under £7,000–£8,000 is around 1.85 per cent with a minimum fee of £20–£25. Lower fees are charged for larger transactions; commission is not charged on new issues. If your stockbroking is "execution only", broker charges will be lower than those of stockbrokers who provide an "advisory" service.

Withdrawals In any amount, at current market price with money back after two to three weeks.

SHARES

Interest — Variable, with dividend paid half-yearly by cheque or direct to your bank account. When shares go ex-dividend, about five weeks before the dividend date, the seller not the buyer receives the next dividend should the shares be sold in that period.

Tax — Dividends are paid net of basic rate tax. The amount deducted, known as the "tax credit", can be reclaimed by non-taxpayers; higher rate taxpayers pay more. Gains made by shareholders are liable to capital gains tax.

Children — Shares bought for a child must be registered in an adult's name.

How to invest — The Stock Exchange will provide names of stockbroking firms willing to take on new clients; but you will receive only limited investment advice unless a) you are an advisory client and are charged more, or b) a discretionary client where the broker manages your portfolio without consulting you first (although you will be informed). Execution-only services (where no advice is given) run by telephone based stockbrokers may offer cheaper deals. Most banks have strengthened their execution-only sharedealing services and several building societies now offer share-dealing as well. Read the City pages and investment magazines for up-to-date information and advice.

Record — Share certificate.

Money Mail Rating — ****! to !!!!!

Investor protection — Share selling is covered by the Financial Services Act, and investors are covered by a compensation scheme of up to £48,000. This does not provide protection against poor shareholdings but unscrupulous selling of shares.

Comment — Share investment is fun and rewarding provided you accept the risk that shares can fall in value, and are also prepared to work at your investments by keeping tabs on share prices and events which might affect your shareholding. Otherwise buy unit trusts or investment trusts and let the managers do the work

SHARES

for you. Preference shares, a fixed interest share investment where the shares rise or fall, are rarely recommended.

Personal Equity Plan

Lump sum or regular savings up to a set limit of £6,000 each year invested in UK shares, companies on the Unlisted Securities Market, unit trusts and investment trusts. Shares quoted in the EU are also now counted as suitable investments for a PEP. A quarter of your PEP (up to £1,500) can be held in non-EU investments. Registered PEP managers, often banks, unit trust groups and stockbrokers, offer investors a choice ranging from one to 10 shares, individual share selection, or a mixture of units and shares or unit trust and investment trusts alone. PEPs are tax free and dividend income can be paid tax free to the PEP holder (not just reinvested). Switching between shares, tax free, is allowed. In addition investors are able to invest £3,000 into a single-company PEP in addition to their main PEP. A Corporate Bond PEP which invests in a range of fixed interest investments (but not gilts) is now available as a PEP option as well.

Suitable for	Long-term build-up of tax-free capital; school fee planning, retirement planning; higher rate taxpayers. Corporate Bond PEPs are suitable for retirement income.
Open to	Anyone 18 or over who does not have a current year PEP.
Min–Max	Varies: £25–£30 a month, £250 lump sum minimum; £500 a month, £6,000 lump sum maximum.
Charges	Initial fee of 0–5 per cent, or £30–£70; annual fees of 1–2 per cent. Additional charges of £20–£35 to attend shareholders' meetings.
Withdrawals	At any time and at current market value.
Interest	Variable.
Tax	Proceeds are free of capital gains tax and dividend income is tax free.
Children	No.

SHARES

How to invest — Offered by stockbrokers, banks, investment trust and unit trust groups. A comprehensive list of PEP managers, their addresses and the investment range and charges of their PEPs is published in the *PEP Investor*. *PEP Guide* lists investment strategy and charges. You need to know your National Insurance number.

Record — Certificate.

Money Mail Rating — ***!! to **!!!

Investor protection — The Financial Services Act covers PEPs, and investors are covered by a compensation scheme of up to £48,000.

Comment — Capital gains tax does not affect many investors, so this particular tax concession only becomes valuable over the long term when other PEPs have been taken out, but it is a flexible form of regular savings compared with life assurance savings and likely to become increasingly popular, for example, for school fees planning, and linked to a mortgage instead of an endowment policy. Check the charges, particularly the level of annual fees and the dealing cost of shares.

Permanent Interest Bearing Shares

Permanent interest bearing shares are quoted and traded on the London Stock Exchange. They are issued by building societies and pay an above-average fixed rate of interest but the value of your capital will go up and down with the price. The shares are irredeemable which means the society does not have to repay the principal. The only way you can get your capital back is to sell the shares. How much you get back depends on the market price of the shares, which can go up and down with demand.

Suitable for — Large investors looking to increase income as part of a portfolio. They are not suitable for savers looking for the best return on their High Street savings.

SHARES

Open to	Anyone.
Min–Max	£1,000; no maximum.
Charges	You pay commission to stockbrokers on buying and selling. The cost is usually 0.5–0.75 per cent, depending on the size of the deal.
Withdrawals	On demand by selling the shares. The proceeds depend on the price at the time of selling.
Interest	Paid out half-yearly. Interest payments are non-cumulative so if the society fails to make a payout, it is under no obligation to make the payment at a future date.
Tax	Interest is paid net of 20 per cent rate tax which can be reclaimed by non-taxpayers. Higher rate tax payers pay more. If you sell the shares at a profit, there is no capital gains tax to pay.
Children	Not suitable.
How to invest	Through a stockbroker.
Record	Share certificate.
Money Mail Rating	**!!!
Investor protection	PIBS are not covered by the building society savings compensation fund. PIBS holders are last in line for a payout if the society is wound up or dissolved.
Comment	PIBS are a relatively new type of share issued by building societies. They offer a high fixed interest but, unlike all other building society investments, your capital is at risk. Unlike ordinary gilt-edged securities, PIBS do not have a redemption date when you get your capital back – as a result their market price is extremely sensitive to the level of interest rates. Initially these shares were aimed at huge investors but recent issues allow for a minimum

purchase of £1,000. Building societies which so far offer PIBS with a low initial investment include Bradford & Bingley (minimum £10,000), Bristol & West, Britannia, Leeds & Holbeck and Skipton, all with a minimum of £1,000.

Shares Quoted on the Alternative Investment Market

Unlike shares which are listed on the Stock Exchange, companies coming to the Alternative Investment Market (AIM) do not have to be as large, as well-established or release as large a proportion of their shares to the public. Dividends are sometimes paid, but the object is to invest for capital gain not income. AIM shares can be included in Personal Equity Plan portfolios of unit trust and investment trust companies (but not in individual's self-select share PEP), and many have moved up to a full listing on the Stock Exchange. The Alternative Investment replaces the Unlisted Securities Market which was closed to new entrants from January 1995. The Alternative Investment Market began in June 1995 to deal in small companies. These companies are vetted by the Stock Exchange, which only regulates the market. Companies will have to nominate an adviser approved by the Stock Exchange to confirm that the company's profits have been checked. Individual investors cannot hold AIM shares directly in a PEP.

Suitable for Investors who wish to build up a long-term stake in new companies; higher rate taxpayers actively avoiding income. Not suitable for "widows and orphans". Investors who, if needs be, can afford to lose their money.

Open to Anyone.

Min–Max Realistic minimum £500; no maximum but with fewer shares available, it is sometimes difficult to buy large amounts.

Charges Stockbroker fees of 1.5–1.65 per cent.

Withdrawals At market price; there will be a larger spread between the buying and selling prices.

SHARES

Interest	Variable, paid net of basic rate tax, and usually low.
Tax	Higher rate taxpayers must pay more on dividends; non-taxpayers can reclaim 20 per cent rate tax deducted; profits are liable to capital gains tax.
Children	Not suitable.
How to invest	Through a stockbroker, but ask his advice; check financial pages for press comment about forthcoming newcomers to the USM.
Record	Share certificate.
Money Mail Rating	**!!! to !!!!!
Investor protection	The Securities Association's compensation fund is now in force. The maximum payout is £48,000.
Comment	Although the casualty rate of USM companies – the predecessors to AIM companes – was not high, their investment performance has been mixed. Companies quoted on AIM are inherently more risky than those quoted on the main Stock Exchange. Consider Venture Capital Trusts, where you have a greater spread of risk, as a long-term alternative. Never buy unquoted shares in foreign companies, and never buy shares from any organisation outside the UK.

Unit Trust

An investment collective: individual unitholders pool their money which is professionally managed and invested in a wide spread of shares and sometimes Government stocks. Unit trust prices mirror the value of the underlying portfolio, and like all equity investments can rise or fall in value. Investors have a choice of investing for income, capital growth or a mixture of both; or you can invest in broadly based general funds covering the entire market spectrum either in the UK or overseas, or combining both, or in specialist funds which concentrate on one country or commercial activity. Unit trusts are now available in a wider range of investments including futures and options, warrants and property.

Suitable for — First time investors in shares; investors wanting to concentrate on one specific overseas investment area; long-term savings for children; investors prepared to sacrifice high immediate income in favour of rising income.

Open to — Anyone.

Min–Max — Commonly £500, sometimes £1,000 minimum. No maximum.

Charges — Initial charge of 3¼–5 per cent built into the "spread", the difference between the buying and selling price of units, which is generally 6–7 per cent. Annual fee of ½–1½ per cent is taken out of the fund's income.

Withdrawals — Managers have to buy back your units and you will receive the current market buying or "bid" price (the lower of the two quoted) with some groups. The quoted price will no longer be the one dealt at, as new rules permit managers to offer "forward pricing" which means that, like investment in shares, you do not know the exact price until after the deal is concluded. Partial withdrawals are possible if a sufficient minimum balance is retained. Sell by telephone, endorse your unit certificate and return to the manager. You will receive your money about a week later.

Interest — Variable, called "distribution" and either paid twice yearly or automatically reinvested if the units are "accumulation" units. A few groups offer monthly income based on a set of unit trusts with different distribution dates.

Tax — Interest is paid net of 20 per cent rate tax. The amount deducted, known as a "tax credit", can be reclaimed by non-taxpayers; higher rate taxpayers pay more. Although a unit trust itself is not liable to capital gains tax, gains made by unitholders are liable to capital gains tax.

Children Units can be held on behalf of a child and are "designated" with the child's name or initials.

How to invest At the end of 1996 there were 163 unit trust management companies running 1,673 unit trusts. Most of these are listed in the national press with addresses and telephone numbers. Managers will send details about any fund. You can buy and sell by phone.

Record A contract note itemising your purchase is followed by a certificate once you have paid for the units.

Money Mail Rating ****! to *!!!!

Investor protection Unitholders' assets are actually held on their behalf by a trustee, usually a major bank or insurance company, formerly approved by the Government but now under the Investment Management Regulatory Organisation (IMRO). In addition each unit trust is authorised by Securities and Investments Board (SIB). The appropriate compensation scheme provides cover up to a maximum of £48,000.

Comment There is a wide variation in investment performance. Unless you are actively prepared to manage your unit trust investments, go first for the broadly based unit trust which you can forget about for years. Specialist funds need careful monitoring: last year's winner is frequently this year's laggard. New unit trusts are often offered at a small discount and tend to perform well initially. Study unit trust "form" in magazine and newspaper articles. Watch charges as they do vary. *Money Management* and *Planned Savings* magazines publish comprehensive performance tables.

Unit Trust or Investment Trust PEP

Modest lump sum or regular savings investment into a personal equity plan invested exclusively in either unit or investment trusts limited to a maximum of £6,000 a year. The proceeds and dividend income are tax free.

Suitable for — First time investors; regular savings; higher rate taxpayers in particular.

Open to — Anyone aged 18 or over who does not already have a current year PEP.

Min–Max — £25–£50 minimum. The lump sum minimum is usually £1,000 but can be lower; maximum £6,000, or £1,500 if you invest in a fund which has less than 50 per cent of its holdings in UK shares at the moment. Some management companies offer a unit trust PEP portfolio which lets the investor hold non-qualifying unit trusts (up to the permitted limit) alongside qualifying funds.

Charges — Vary. Usually normal unit trust charges and no extras. Others are experimenting with no initial fees, but imposing a charge if you encash the PEP within the first three years.

Withdrawals — At any time and at current market value; partial withdrawals may be permitted.

Interest — Variable.

Tax — The proceeds are free of capital gains tax and interest is tax free.

Children — No.

How to invest — Phone or write to unit trust and investment trust management groups for details. Compare charges in specialist publications such as *PEP Guide*. You need to know your National Insurance number.

Record — Certificate.

SHARES

Money Mail Rating	***!! to **!!!
Investor protection	The Financial Services Act includes PEPs, and investors are covered by a compensation scheme of up to £48,000.
Comment	PEPs should be the first form of unit trust investment for most people. Check that there is little or no element of double charging in respect of PEP and unit trust fees. Remember, you will need to know your National Insurance number when applying for any PEP. Husbands and wives cannot jointly own a PEP, but each can individually take one out.

Unit Trust Savings Scheme

A regular savings scheme for an unlimited period into a unit trust (see page **143**). Flexible: additional savings can be made at any time; savings can be stopped at any time, and either sold in part or together, or held as a lump sum investment. Minimum monthly savings can be very small.

Suitable for	Savers who cannot afford the minimum lump sum investment in unit trusts; regular savers building up capital from income.
Open to	Anyone.
Min–Max	Commonly £30–£40, sometimes £50 a month. No maximum.
Charges	Initial charge of 3¼–5 per cent is built into the "spread", the difference of 6–7 per cent between the buying and selling price of units. Annual fee of ½–1½ per cent is taken out of the fund's income.
Withdrawals	Managers have to buy back your units and you will receive the current market buying or "bid" price. Partial withdrawals are sometimes allowed. You will receive your money about a week later.
Interest	Variable, and either accumulated within the units or used to buy extra units.
Tax	Interest is paid net of 20 per cent rate tax. The amount deducted, known as a "tax credit", can be

reclaimed by non-taxpayers; higher rate taxpayers must pay more. Unitholders are liable to capital gains tax.

Children Units can be held on behalf of a child and are designated with child's name or initials.

How to invest Most of the major unit trust groups run a monthly savings plan; newer groups formed by insurance companies and most of the stockbroker unit trust groups might not have a regular savings plan. Ask managers for an application form.

Record Half-yearly statement of interest and the number of units bought each period sent.

Money Mail Rating ****! to *!!!!

Investor protection Unitholders' assets are actually held on their behalf by a trustee, usually a major bank or insurance company; formerly approved by the Government but now under IMRO, the Investment Management Regulatory Organisation. In addition each unit trust is authorised by SIB, the Securities and Investments Board, which has a compensation scheme providing cover of up to a maximum of £48,000.

Comment Regular purchases of units helps to iron out fluctuations in unit prices. Investors who believe in investment cycles should use a savings scheme to buy plenty of units in a specialist fund while the price is low at the bottom of the cycle. Otherwise stick to a general fund for a longer term investment. A unit trust savings scheme may be cheaper, initially, than a monthly savings plan into a unit trust PEP, although over the long term the PEP will probably be the more rewarding investment.

Venture Capital Trust

A form of investment trust which invests in a spread of smaller, often unquoted companies, which the Government encourages by giving investors tax breaks to back them. Investment of up to £100,000 receives 20 per cent tax relief.

The kind of companies selected by venture capital trust managers in the main are not business start-ups, which are considered to be the most risky, but companies which are already up-and-running and need usually to raise capital for further expansion. VCT managers have up to three years to find suitable investments and they can invest in shares already quoted on the Alternative Investment Market (see page 142).

Suitable for	Investors who are comfortable with risk investments. Higher rate taxpayers and investors who have a capital gains tax liability and wish to defer the tax bill. Not suitable for nervous or saftey first investors.
Open to	Anyone.
Min–Max	Minimum investment usually £2,000–£3,000; maximum qualifying for tax relief, £100,000.
Charges	Initial charges typically 5 per cent; annual charge 1.0–2.5 per cent.
Withdrawals	Any time, but tax benefits are cancelled if investment sold within five years.
Interest	Variable.
Tax	Tax relief at 20 per cent is given on the first £100,000 invested provided investment is held for five years; dividend income is tax free; investors can defer the capital gains liability on another investment(s) if the proceeds are reinvested in a VCT.
Children	Not suitable.
How to invest	Independent financial advisers and stockbrokers will have details. A new fund will issue a prospectus, published in the personal finance section of many newspapers. Existing funds are bought through a stockbroker.
Record	Share certificate.
Money Mail Rating	*!!!! to !!!!!

SHARES

Investor Protection

Trust managers are regulated by the IMRO which has a compensation scheme providing cover up to a maximum of £48,000.

Comment

VCTs are risk investments, but at least you have a spread of investments unlike an EIS which is a one-company investment. It is a practical way of deferring a capital gains tax liability, but even so, investors should not have too high a proportion of their money in this kind of investment.

CHAPTER 20

Stocks

Bond Fund

Unit trusts which invest in Government stock and equivalent bonds issued by other Governments overseas are usually described as Bond Funds rather than Bond Unit Trusts. They function exactly like unit trusts, and despite being restricted to fixed interest stocks have shown some strong capital growth too. (When interest rates in general fall, the capital value of Gilts and the like tends to increase.) Bond funds concentrating on Corporate Bonds (see Loan and Debenture, page 156) can be held in a PEP.

Suitable for	Cautious investors and those who are seeking more rather than less income from their investments.
Open to	Anyone.
Min–Max	Varies, but a minimum of £1,000 is common.
Charges	An initial charge of around 5 per cent is built into the "spread", the difference between the buying and selling price of units. There is also an annual fee of 1–1.5 per cent.
Withdrawals	On demand, at the lower (or bid) price of the units.
Interest	Variable, usually distributed half yearly.

STOCKS

Tax — Distribution is net of 20 per cent rate tax; non-taxpayers can reclaim the tax paid, but higher rate taxpayers will pay more. Unitholders are liable to capital gains tax on profits made.

Children — Units can be held on behalf of a child.

How to invest — Most management groups advertise their funds in the national press. Alternatively, use the services of an independent financial adviser to recommend a fund which best suits your needs.

Record — A certificate.

Money Mail Rating — ***** to ****!

Investor Protection — Fund management groups are regulated under the terms of the Financial Services Act. A compensation scheme provides cover up to a maximum of £48,000.

Comment — Bond Funds tend to perform well at different times to funds invested in ordinary shares, so can be a complementary investment to mainstream unit trusts. Their income and safety-first qualities make them an attractive choice for cautious investors, but you can only get the tax advantages of a PEP with funds specialising in Corporate Bonds.

Government Index-Linked

Government index-linked stocks are identical to fixed interest Government stocks except in two very important respects. Instead of paying a fixed rate of interest, a modest fixed rate of interest is increased over each six month period in line with increases in the Retail Price Index. At the end of the stock's fixed life span, the nominal value repaid is also increased in line with increases in the Retail Price Index since its issue.

Suitable for — Anyone wishing to protect their capital from inflation; for higher rate taxpayers, the yields are not high and the stocks are bought for capital appreciation.

STOCKS

Open to	Anyone.
Min–Max	See Government Stock.
Charges	See Government Stock.
Withdrawals	Any amount at the current market price which will not mirror, at this stage, changes in the Retail Price Index; if withdrawn at redemption, the price will reflect increase in Retail Price Index since the stock was issued.
Interest	Variable, and will reflect changes in the Retail Price Index over a six month period. See Government Stock for "ex-dividend".
Tax	See Government Stock.
Children	See Government Stock.
How to invest	See Government Stock.
Record	Stock certificate.
Money Mail Rating	***** if held to redemption, otherwise ****!
Investor protection	Guaranteed by the Government; the Securities Association compensation scheme provides cover up to a maximum of £48,000.
Comment	In periods of relatively low inflation these stocks have not performed as well as conventional fixed interest stocks, but are likely to improve their rating if inflation rises. National Savings index-linked certificates could be a better medium- to short-term investment although maximum investment is limited.

Index-Linked Stock

	(a)
2% Treasury 1996	67.9
2½% Treasury 2001	78.3
2½% Treasury 2003	78.8
2% Treasury 2006	69.5
2½% Treasury 2009	78.8
2½% Treasury 2011	74.6
2½% Treasury 2013	89.2
2½% Treasury 2016	81.6
2½% Treasury 2020	83.0
2½% Treasury 2024	97.7
4½% Treasury 2030	135.1

(a) *RPI base month for index-linking adjusted to reflect rebasing of RPI to 100 in January 1987.*

Government Stock

(Commonly called Gilt-Edged Securities)

A lump sum investment in a stock issued by the Government as part of its fund-raising programme. Most stocks are issued with a fixed interest rate and a fixed life span, at the end of which the Government will redeem them in full, at the "nominal" value.

The yield, the return the investor gets from stock at that price, is the yardstick for investing in gilts. If interest rates in general fall, higher-yielding stock will be in demand and the stock price will rise, ultimately driving the yield down; conversely if interest rates are rising, investors will sell their gilts (to get a better return elsewhere) and the price of the stock will fall, forcing the yield up. When you see gilts quoted in the press, you will often see two yields: one is the straight interest/price yield, the other, the "net redemption" yield, takes into account the capital gain or loss, averaged out, that you would make if the stock were held to redemption.

Suitable for Most taxpayers, who should buy stocks appropriate to their tax bracket; higher rate taxpayers will be more interested in capital gains while the high yield on other stocks makes them a suitable investment for a retirement portfolio.

Open to Anyone.

STOCKS

Min–Max Theoretically no minimum, but £250–£500 is more practical in view of the commission to be paid. No maximum, except for stock bought from the National Savings Stock Register where the maximum daily purchase of any one stock is £10,000.

Charges On gilts bought from the National Savings Stock Register (via your local post office), the charges are cheaper than buying through a stockbroker. The charges for buying gilts through a stockbroker or bank vary, ranging from 0.4 per cent up to £20,000 to 1.5 per cent up to £5,000. Shop around. There are no charges if you buy a new issue or when the stock is redeemed.

Withdrawals Any amount at the current market price; or at redemption date.

Interest Fixed, paid half-yearly, net of basic rate tax if bought through a stockbroker or bank, except for War Loan where dividends are always without deduction of tax. If bought from the National Savings Stock Register, dividends are paid gross. Stocks go ex-dividend about five weeks before the dividend date, with the interest going to the seller not the buyer. This is reflected in the price as the interest due to the next dividend date is subtracted from the stock price.

Tax Investors who pay tax at the basic rate are liable to 20 per cent tax on the gross dividend payment from stock on the National Savings Stock Register; higher rate taxpayers must pay more on dividends from stock bought through a stockbroker or bank where 20 per cent tax is deducted at source; non-taxpayers can reclaim the tax. Gilts are exempt from capital gains tax.

Children Stock bought through stockbrokers or banks must be in an adult's name; stock from the National Savings Stock Register can be in the child's name. Children's holdings cannot be transferred to the Bank of England's Stock Register until they are 18.

How to invest Through a stockbroker or bank for stock held on the Bank of England Stock Register – this is a comprehensive list. All issues of Government stock

STOCKS

are now held on the National Savings Stock Register for which application forms for purchase are available at your post office. The form is DNS 400 (GS1); repurchase forms and envelopes are also available at the post office.

Record	Stock certificate.
Money Mail Rating	***** if held to redemption, otherwise ****!
Investor protection	Guaranteed by the Government; the Securities Association compensation scheme, providing up to £48,000, is now in force.
Comment	Dealing through a stockbroker or bank will give you a more immediate price; you might get the next or an even later day's price on purchases from the National Savings Stock Register. But the dealing costs are cheaper and interest is paid without deduction of tax. It is possible to switch from one register to another: obtain the forms from either the Bank of England or Bonds and Stock Office, Blackpool FY3 9YP.

Loan and Debenture (Corporate Bonds)

A lump sum investment in a stock issued by a company at a fixed rate of interest over a fixed period. At the end of the period, the stock is redeemed in full, but until that point the stock is at market prices which can rise or fall. As with Government fixed rate stock, company stock is quoted with a net redemption yield, reflecting any capital gains or losses to be made from that point until maturity, as well as the interest return. Some loan stocks are convertible into ordinary shares at a fixed date and price. The arrival of Corporate Bond PEPs means that more companies are issuing this stock.

Suitable for	Most taxpayers whether they want income or capital growth.
Open to	Anyone aged 18 or over.

STOCKS

Min–Max	Realistic minimum £1,000–£2,000; no maximum.
Charges	A stockbroker's typical commission is 0.9 per cent on the first £5,000, 0.45 per cent on the next £5,000, less on larger amounts. No fees are levied on new issues or on redemption.
Withdrawals	Any amount at market value; or at redemption date.
Interest	Fixed, paid half-yearly with 20 per cent rate tax deducted. Stock goes ex-dividend about five weeks before interest is paid which means the seller, not buyer, keeps the interest, although the price is adjusted downwards accordingly.
Tax	Higher rate taxpayers must pay more, non-taxpayers can reclaim tax deducted. Stocks are exempt from capital gains tax.
Children	In an adult's name.
How to invest	Through a stockbroker or bank; check convertible options, redemption dates and long-term outlook for the company before proceeding.
Record	Stock certificate.
Money Mail Rating	****! to ***!!
Investor protection	If a company fails, debenture holders have a prior claim to be paid in full ahead of other creditors. The Securities Association's compensation scheme, maximum compensation £48,000, is now in force.
Comment	Stick to well-known companies; the convertible option can be an attractive way of building up an equity portfolio later. Consider a Corporate Bond PEP so that you can receive tax-free income.

Appendix 1

Shareholder Perks

Many companies give perks to shareholders based on the number of shares owned. Some are more attractive and worthwhile than others; but none should be considered as the reason for buying the shares in the first place. Treat the perk as a welcome bonus instead.

The following list, detailing perks by type, and then itemising the individual companies and minimum shareholding to qualify, is based on information supplied by stockbrokers and financial advisers Hargreaves Lansdown.

*If your shares are held in a nominee account with your stockbroker, make sure the company in which you are investing will issue the perks to you.

Cars – Accessories, Distributors, etc.

ALEXANDERS HOLDINGS *2,000*
Shareholders' special discount of around 2 per cent is available, in normal trading circumstances, on any new vehicle bought from one of the Alexanders dealerships based in Edinburgh, Kirkintilloch, Greenock, and Northampton. The discount will be over and above any other discount available. This company is a Ford dealer.

ARMOUR TRUST *All shareholders*
Discounts up to 20 per cent on car valeting through Autosheen.

KWIK-FIT HOLDINGS plc *100 ordinary*
Shareholders are entitled to a 10 per cent discount on two purchases each year of £5 or over. The full price is payable on purchase and a 10 per cent refund will be returned to the shareholder by post.

LEX SERVICE *All Shareholders*
Occasionally special offers sent to shareholders e.g. MOT and reduced price servicing and discounts on the purchase of a new car.

LOOKERS GROUP *All private registered holders of ordinary shares*
Shareholders are entitled to a £100 discount on the normal price on the purchase of any new motor vehicle purchased from any one of the company's garages. This discount is over and above any discounts negotiated in the usual way. The range of vehicles includes Rover, Vauxhall, Ford, Mercedes, VW, Audi, Toyota, Renault, Diahatsu, Peugeot, Nissan, Hyundai and Seat.

PERRY GROUP *All Shareholders*
Privilege purchase terms are available on new cars. Deals will be struck on an individual basis and

shareholders should telephone Mr Hickman-Ashby 01992–554188. Perry's also offer a 10 per cent discount on vehicle rental, 10 per cent on car servicing and mechanical repairs and 10 per cent on parts and accessories purchased at a Perry's part shop. A card, available on request, must be produced when claiming discount.

QUICKS *500 shares*

Vouchers are issued to shareholders entitling them to discount at Quicks outlets on service, vehicle accessories and new vehicles. Voucher booklet available on request.

Confectionery

THORNTONS *200 ordinary*

Discount vouchers are sent to shareholders on the register at the time of the Annual Report in October. In 1995 the value of the vouchers was £21, and there are no plans at present to change this arrangement.

DIY

BERISFORD plc *100 ordinary shares held in shareholders own name*

Qualifying shareholders are issued with a Magnet Privilege Card entitling them to the following discounts on Magnet goods: LIST PRICE LESS 50 per cent for Magnet produced kitchen and bedroom items, LIST PRICE LESS 40 per cent for Magnet produced joinery items, LIST PRICE LESS 20 per cent for bought in items such as appliances, sinks, taps and tiles.

MEYER INTERNATIONAL *250 ordinary*

Private shareholders are issued with a Jewson discount card entitling the holder to 10 per cent off any purchases, except sale items, from any branch of Jewson. Branches stock a wide range of buildings materials, timber and DIY items.

NORCROS *500 ordinary*

Shareholders are entitled to a 10 per cent discount on retail purchases of Norcros Group products valued at £20 or more. Application for a discount must be supported by a letter from the shareholder stating that the goods have been purchased for their personal use. The following companies are part of the Norcros Group:
Building Adhesives Ltd – adhesives, grouts etc; Crosby Kitchens – fitted kitchens; Grosby Sarek Ltd – timber doors and windows; H & R Johnson Tiles Ltd – ceramic wall & floor tiles; Triton plc – electric showers etc.

Dry Cleaning

BROOKS SERVICE GROUP *750 ordinary*

Shareholders will be issued with a concession card which entitles the bearer to: 25 per cent discount on all services, including dry cleaning, tailoring and repairs, shoe repairs, key cutting, shirt service, photo processing, laundry, curtain cleaning, duvet cleaning, hire of carpet cleaning equipment and bridal gown care. No order can be the subject of more than one price concession. Discounts will not be available on seasonal or other special offers. Cards will be issued to each shareholder and will expire on 30 November, at which point a new card will be issued to qualifying shareholders.

JOHNSON GROUP CLEANERS *200 ordinary shares/ 1,000 preference shares or 10p convertible preference shares*

Shareholders who are eligible will receive a discount card entitling them to 25 per cent off all dry cleaning at Johnson Group shops. Johnson Group Cleaners group include Johnsons, Smiths, Crockatt Cleaning, Pullars, Bollom, Zernys, Hartonclean, Harris Clean, and Kneels.

SHARPE & FISHER *All shareholders*

10 vouchers sent out with annual report in May, each allowing £5 off any purchase of £100 or more.

SKETCHLEY *1,000 ordinary*

A shareholder's discount card is issued which entitles the holder to 25 per cent discount off list prices at Sketchley Cleaners for most services. 10 per cent discount off photocopying at SupaSnaps and 10 per cent discount off all items at Sketchley and SupaSnap branches. To qualify for perks the shares must be registered in the shareholder's and not a nominee name.

Fashion

AUSTIN REED *500 ordinary shares*
Shareholders can apply for a Shareholder Discount Card which entitles them to 15 per cent discount on purchases of ladies and menswear and most other merchandise at the company's retail outlets. This offer cannot be used in conjunction with any other special offers, and applies to cash or credit sales charges to an Austin Reed account.

BURTON GROUP *1,000 ordinary held in shareholders own name*
A 12.5 per cent discount is available on most goods bought in the group's retail outlets using a Shareholder discount credit card. The reduction is automatically shown on the monthly statement. This discount is limited to the first £5,000 worth of eligible purchases per annum in the groups financial year (1st September–31 August). Therefore the maximum annual discount is £625. The groups retail outlets include Burtons, Debenhams, Dorothy Perkins, Evans, Principles, Top Man, and Top Shop. For details and an application form shareholders need to contact the company on 0113 2365665.

COATS VIYELLA *All Shareholders*
Two vouchers are issued to all shareholders with the Annual Report around April. To receive these, shareholders must be on the register when the report is sent out. The vouchers entitle the shareholder to a 20 per cent discount on purchases on one occasion in any freestanding Jaeger store and on one occasion in any freestanding Viyella store. It can be used for both ladies and menswear. It is not valid in conjunction with any other offer. The company reviews its practice of issuing vouchers on an annual basis.

GIEVES GROUP *600 ordinary shares (held for a minimum of 3 months)*
Shareholders are issued with a card which entitles them to a 10 per cent discount on purchases made in Gieves & Hawkes' UK stores. Discount will not be allowed on goods purchased with other credit or charge cards. Discount does not include purchases from the Company's concession and overseas outlets. Shares cannot be held in a nominee name to qualify for discounts.

THE HOLLAS GROUP *500 ordinary*
Shareholders are offered a 20 per cent discount on goods purchased at the associated company of Hawkshead Sportswear Ltd, at its four retail outlets in Hawkshead and Grasmere in Cumbria and King Edward Court at Windsor.

LAURA ASHLEY *All Shareholders*
A voucher allowing 15 per cent discount on one purchase has been sent to shareholders along with the Annual Report and Accounts in the last few years. The voucher is valid for use in the UK and North America.

MOSS BROS GROUP *250 ordinary shares (held for a minimum of 6 months)*
Shareholders are entitled to a 10 per cent discount at the company's retail outlets. The discount does not apply to items "on sale".

NEXT *500 shares*
A discount voucher was sent with the 1995 Annual Report and Accounts to qualifying shareholders. The voucher entitled the shareholder or his/her immediate family to a 25 per cent discount from the price of all purchases made at any one time at any branch of Next. The voucher was valid until the 30th September 1995, and could not be used in conjunction with any other discount voucher or to buy sale merchandise, or at any branch of Next to Nothing, or at Next Directory.

SEARS plc *500 ordinary shares*
The scheme is available to UK residents who are individual shareholders, registered in their own names on 16th May 1994. A Shareholder Privilege card for use by qualifying shareholders and their immediate family is provided to obtain discounts in

all departments of Selfridges, Selfridge Selection mail order catalogue, most Sears UK retail outlets and Freemans mail order catalogue. A total saving of £500 against purchases of £5,000 is possible. Sears plc donate 20 pence to Save the Children Fund for every £1 of discount used, up to a maximum donation of £50,000. The scheme is valid until 31 May 1996. A decision regarding 1996 will be announced on publication of the Annual Report for 1995–6.

Financial Services

ABERDEEN TRUST *2,000 ordinary*
Qualifying shareholders are entitled to free membership of The Country Gentlemen's Association. The benefits of the Association include an annual diary, the monthly magazine "Country" and various special offers in the areas of travel, wine, etc. All qualifying shareholders are entitled to a 2 per cent discount on the purchase of units in certain unit trusts in the Abtrust range of unit trusts.

BANK OF SCOTLAND *1,200 ordinary shares or £2,500 nominal in Bank's preference stock held for at least 12 months*
The Bank of Scotland Personal Stockholders Benefits Scheme covers four products: 1. Premier Visa Card. The enrolment fee and annual subscription are waived for shareholders who comply with the required criteria. 2. One-third off Bank of Scotland's Travel Insurance and 12.5% discount on annual travel insurance premium. 3. 50 per cent discount on normal Bank of Scotland PEP management charges. 4. Bank of Scotland Visa traveller's cheques are available free of their normal commission charge.

BERRY BIRCH & NOBLE *500 ordinary*
10 per cent discount off premium (after all policy discounts) of any household insurance policies, in respect of your main residence, effected through the agency of the company. The company is informed when a policy is effected or renewed.

GENERAL ACCIDENT *All Shareholders*
Shareholders and their immediate family living with them are entitled to a discount of 10 per cent on personal insurance policies effected directly with General Accident through their local branch. A concession is also available on certain life policies depending on the nature of the contract and length of term. The discount does not apply to nominee accounts.

INVESCO plc *All Shareholders*
Shareholders are entitled to a discount of approximately 2 per cent of the initial charge in respect of all unit trusts and PEP investments.

Foods

ICELAND FROZEN FOODS *All Shareholders*
Food vouchers are normally issued to all shareholders with the Company's Interim Reports in September. The vouchers are: £1 voucher off per £10 spent on groceries. £2 voucher off £20 spent on groceries. £3 voucher off £30 spent on groceries. £10 voucher off £100 spent on appliances.

PARK FOOD GROUP *All Shareholders*
Park Food Group offers shareholders a 20 per cent discount on their Park Premier Collection range of hampers.

Furnishing

COURTS plc *100 ordinary shares held for a minimum of 3 months*
Shareholders are entitled to a discount of 10 per cent on purchases at Courts retail outlets. This may not apply to concessions operating within the stores.

LYLES (S) plc *500 ordinary shares*
15 per cent discount on carpets in the mill shop at Calder Bank Mills, Dewsbury, West Yorkshire.

EMESS *All Shareholders*
A 30 per cent discount on the retail price of Brilliant UK range of table lamps. Brilliant supplies direct to retailers and purchase of products must be direct from the company.

ESSEX FURNITURE *2,500 shares*
A 15 per cent discount is allowed on furniture purchased at any of their stores.

WORLD OF LEATHER plc *500 ordinary shares held for a minimum of 6 months*
A 10 per cent discount is available on all World of Leather products and may be taken in addition to any other offers operating at the time.

Health

COMMUNITY HOSPITALS GROUP *500 ordinary*
Shareholders living near facilities are invited to hospitality events such as the launching of a new service or opening of a new extension. The HealthCheck range of health screens is available at a 20 per cent discount to shareholders. Priority reservations are given to shareholders and close relations. Shareholders admitted to any of the hospitals are welcomed with a hospitality gift pack.

LLOYDS CHEMIST GROUP *All Shareholders*
Two 20 per cent discount vouchers with an expiry date are issued to all shareholders with the Company's annual report and accounts and interim statement. These can be used at any of the group's stores; Lloyds Chemists, Lloyds Supersave Drugstores, Holland and Barrett, Lloyds Eyecare Centres and John Bell and Croyden.

REGINA plc *2,000, or any number but registered prior to 6/9/91 ord*
Shareholders are entitled to a 25 per cent discount on the company's products including special offers and pre-launch lines. This discount is available on mail order purchases only. Mailings are made to registered shareholders regularly throughout the year.

SPECIALEYES plc *All Shareholders*
Shareholders are offered a discount of 10 per cent on one transaction involving the purchase of one or more pairs of complete spectacles. The application should be made in writing to the Company Secretary indicating your nearest branch.

Hotels

BURTONWOOD BREWERY *All Shareholders*
Discount vouchers to the following values were issued in 1995 and the company intend to make similar offers in the future: £25 off a weekend break package at listed hotels; £12 off a meal for two or more at listed Burtonwood pubs; 2 × £4 off bar snacks for two or more at listed Burtonwood pubs.

FORTE *80 Granada shares (as Forte has been taken over by Granada)*
A shareholder concession of 12.5 per cent discount is available through either the Forte Gold Card or through Leisure Cheques. If the Forte Gold Card is used the 12.5 per cent discount will be shown on the monthly statement not at the outlet. The Leisure Cheques can be bought at 90 per cent of their face value which gives a 10 per cent discount. They are then used at face value, and no further discount is available on use. Further information 0171–240 2040 (0181–568 4540 Gold Card information).

FRIENDLY HOTELS *All Shareholders*
A Friendly Club card is issued to all shareholders entitling the holder to 10 per cent off the published hotel accommodation tariff and Short Break Weekends at any Friendly Hotels. Spouse rate is also available – a twin or double room for the price of a single. Other discounts are notified as they become available.

THE GREENALLS GROUP *All Shareholders*
Shareholders qualify for all year round discounts on De Vere hotels. 20 per cent off the current accommodation rate at any De Vere Hotel. 10 per cent off De Vere Leisure Breaks. 10 per cent off the Before you Fly package. Shareholders also receive 10 per cent off the first year's membership fee on De Vere Leisureclubs. Also special shareholder's

breaks are available which give discounted rates at varying hotels for certain periods, which include dinner, bed and breakfast. Shareholders are also given special offers on Berkeley Wines.

JURYS HOTEL GROUP plc *All shareholders on register by 20/7/95*
Discount card allowing 10 per cent on accommodation charges and meals at any of the group's hotels and restaurants.

LADBROKE GROUP *All Shareholders*
Shareholders are entitled to discounts as follows: 10 per cent off room tariffs, food and beverages in Hilton UK and overseas hotels, (NB 10 per cent off food and beverages in overseas hotels only when resident at the hotel). 20 per cent off pre-booked Short Breaks. 10 per cent off pre-booked Special Interest and Action Extra Breaks. 5 per cent off published conference package tariffs. Free upgrade to Executive or Plaza accommodation on arrival at UK Hilton hotels (if available).

QUEENS MOAT HOUSES *Minimum 1,000 ordinary shares*
The current shareholder concession is for £40 made up of a £25 voucher towards the cost of a Town & Country Classic Weekend Break and 2 × £7.50 vouchers towards food and beverage costs.

RYAN HOTELS *All Shareholders*
10 per cent discount on accommodation, food and beverages at any of the group's hotels.

THE SAVOY HOTELS *All Shareholders*
A 10 per cent discount on accommodation at the Savoy, Claridge's, The Connaught, The Berkeley and The Lygon Arms. The discount cannot be used in conjunction with any other promotional offers, and does not apply to food and drink. Reservations can be made either through the central reservations office, telephone 0171–872 8080, or to the hotel direct.

SECURICOR GROUP *All Shareholders*
The Securicor Group offers shareholders 10 per cent discount at the group's hotels in Richmond and Coventry and 5 per cent discount on package holidays booked through Phoenix Travel. A free buffet lunch is also provided for shareholders attending the AGM in April.

STAKIS *Minimum of 300 shares*
Shareholders are entitled to a 30 per cent discount on their overnight accommodation bill when booking at the published rack rate – and 20 per cent off the booking price when booking at the published rates in the Stakis Holidays and Short Breaks brochure. Even when shareholders are not staying in the hotel, they are still entitled to 20 per cent off their bill if they are eating in a Stakis restaurant. There is also a 10 per cent discount on Leisure Club membership.

VAUX GROUP *All Shareholders*
A discount card is issued to shareholders each calendar year. This entitles the bearer to 10 per cent off accommodation and restaurant bills at Swallow Hotels, 10 per cent off meals at Vaux Inns and 10 per cent off annual membership at Swallow Leisure Clubs. The group also issue vouchers towards the cost of weekend breaks.

Jewellery

ASPREY *5,062 ordinary*
An Asprey Card entitles shareholders to 15 per cent discount on cash and cheque purchases from any of the Asprey Group Stores. This discount is not given for repairs or valuations.

GOLDSMITHS GROUP *All Shareholders*
The company issues its shareholders with 2 × 15 per cent discount vouchers every 6 months to be used against any single purchases. The vouchers cannot be used in conjunction with any other promotional offer.

SIGNET GROUP *All 10p ordinary shareholders and 6.875p convertible preference shareholders*
A shareholder discount card is issued which entitles shareholders to 10 per cent discount on all goods and services throughout the UK. Retail outlets include H Samuel, Ernest Jones and Leslie Davis.

Miscellaneous

AMBERLEY GROUP plc *10,000 ordinary*
The company is prepared to offer a 15 per cent discount on the products and services it offers in the French and Belgian markets.

GRANADA GROUP *All shareholders*
No perks are being offered to shareholders this year, and the situation is being reviewed for next year. However for the benefit of shareholders there is a low cost dealing service, a PEP and a share dividend scheme.

LONRHO *100 ordinary shares held by 1st March 1994 or earlier*
Various discounts on jewellery, watches and clocks at Southern Watch & Clock Supplies.

PENTOS *500 ordinary*
Shareholders are entitled to 10 per cent discount in all Pentos' retail outlets, i.e. Dillons, Claude Gill, Hatchards, Economist, Athena and Ryman.

PSION plc *1,000 shares*
Discount of 15 per cent, limited to one machine per year.

THOMAS JOURDAN *1,000 ordinary shares held for a minimum of 6 months*
Discounts are available from the following retail outlets: John Corby Ltd – Trouser presses, Tie Presses, Lion Brush Ltd – Artists & Cosmetic brushes approx 30 per cent, Suncrest Surrounds Ltd – Fireplace surrounds & suites, approx. 25 per cent; Unerman Holdings plc – Furniture fittings, handles, etc approx 20 per cent.

Photography

UPTON & SOUTHERN HOLDINGS *250 ordinary*
Shareholders are entitled to receive discounts on purchases from the company's retail outlet E Upton & Sons plc in the Cleveland and Yorkshire areas. They are sent a discount card for this purpose. The discounts available are 10 per cent–15 per cent but do not apply to sale goods.

Property

BARRATT DEVELOPMENTS *1,000 ordinary shares held for a continuous period of 12 months prior to legal completion of purchase*
Barratt shareholders are entitled to special discount terms when purchasing a Barratt property in the UK, or USA. When buying a new or part exchange home from any of their housebuilding companies, shareholders are entitled to a discount of £500 for every £25,000 (or part thereof) of the purchase price. A discount is also available when purchasing or renting leisure property at any of the Group's resorts in Britain and Europe. You must inform the Sales Representative on site when reserving your property that you are claiming shareholder's discount.

BELLWAY *Varies according to concession as below*
1. Bellair Car Port: the company operates a car parking facility for people flying from Newcastle Airport. If shareholders wish to use this a discount of 10 per cent is given off normal prices in the summer (mid April to mid November) rising to 50 per cent in the winter season (mid November to mid April). To qualify you must have been the registered holder of 1,000 ordinary shares for six months prior to reservation of car parking space. 2. Should shareholders wish to purchase kitchen units from their subsidiary Nixons Kitchens they are entitled to a discount of 10 per cent off normal list prices. To qualify you must have been the registered holder of 1,000 ordinary shares for six months. 3. Should shareholders wish to purchase a new Bellway house they are entitled to a discount of £600 per £25,000 or pro rata on part thereof, of the purchase price to a maximum of £3,000. To qualify you must have been the registered holder of 2,000 ordinary shares for 12 months prior to the reservation of your new home. You must also inform the sales representative on site when reserving your property that you are claiming shareholder discount.

FIRED EARTH TILES *500 ordinary shares held for a minimum of 6 months*
Shareholders are entitled to a 12 per cent discount on the company's products.

McCARTHY & STONE plc *500 ordinary shares for continuous 12 months prior to legal completion of purchase*
Shareholders, subject to the above, are entitled to a discount of £1,000 per property, or the equivalent in foreign currency, when buying a McCarthy & Stone property in Britain, France or Southern Ireland. This is in addition to any other general discount being advertised at the time. In the UK the offer applies only to retirement properties. You must inform the Sales Consultant on the site when reserving your property that you are claiming shareholder's discount.

PERSIMMON plc *500 shares*
1 per cent discount to shareholders off the price of its new and part-exchange properties. You must inform the Sales Negotiator on site when reserving your home that you are claiming the shareholders discount.

Publishing

EMAP *All Shareholders*
Discounted subscriptions have been offered on various consumer magazines, e.g. Practical Photography, Garden News, Steam Railways, Car, Choice, and Empire.

REED INTERNATIONAL plc *All shareholders*
Discount offers on Reed Elsevier's consumer magazines and books.

Restaurants

ALLIED DOMECQ *All Shareholders*
A book of vouchers is issued to shareholders each year, offering discounts on company products. In 1994–95 these included discounts for dining at specified restaurants, offers at Victoria Wine on a range of spirits, wine, and beer, and various prize draws and offers on days out; ie sponsored events.

CITY CENTRE RESTAURANTS *All Shareholders*
The company includes discount vouchers within its Annual Report and Accounts for its restaurants. These include Garfunkel's, Deep Pan Pizza Co, Chiquito, Filling Station, Cafe Uno, Adams Rib, Zacks, Nachos and Frankie & Benny's.

GROUPE CHEZ GERARD *All Shareholders*
All shareholders for 1995 were given 5 wine vouchers with the 1995 annual report and accounts. Each voucher allows them a free bottle of house wine or a discount worth the same amount towards a more expensive bottle of wine when dining in one of the company's restaurants – Chez Gerard, Bertorelli's, Cafe Fish, Soho Soho, Scotts and Chutney Mary. Shareholders will also be offered, at the time of the interim report, 2 restaurant vouchers worth £25 each to give them, plus a guest the opportunity to try the company's restaurants.

HARRY RAMSDEN'S plc *500 ordinary shares*
A "Shareholder's Card" entitles the bearer and one guest to 20 per cent discount on restaurant meals served from Monday to Friday inclusive (excluding bank holidays) at any of the company's outlets. Invitations will also be extended to shareholders to functions held at the original Harry Ramsden's in Guiseley – "the worlds largest fish and chip shop" where celebrities will also be in attendance.

MY KINDA TOWN plc *2,500 shares as at 1/7/95*
Shareholders will receive a Golden Guest Card which entitles them to 20 per cent off their lunch or dinner bills when two or more people dine at any of My Kinda Town's 46 restaurants around the world. Holders of the Golden Guest Card will automatically enter the annual draw for the World Traveller Award. The prize is a trip for two to one of the sixteen countries where My Kinda Town is represented. The winners choice will include Bangkok, Buenos Aires, Barcelona or, if they wish, a gateway city in the United States of America.

Retailing

ARGOS plc *All shareholders*
A discount voucher has historically been sent to all registered shareholders in August, with the Company's interim report. This has entitled shareholders to a once-off discount depending on the amount of sale transaction (ie £2 on a purchase of £20–£40, £4 on a purchase of £40.01–£60, £6 on a purchase of £60.01–£100, £10 on a purchase of £100.01–£150, £15 on a purchase of over £150). Vouchers have a limited life – in 1995 they were valid until November 26th, and they can only be used against a purchase of merchandise (not gift vouchers or postal purchases). A decision on whether to offer a voucher and the level of discount given is taken on a year by year basis.

BENTALLS *100 ordinary*
The company issues shareholders with six discount vouchers along with the Annual Report and Accounts. These entitle shareholders to a £1 to £10 discount against 10 per cent of the bill in any of the company's seven department stores based in London and the South East.

THE BOOTS COMPANY *100 ordinary*
For the past few years shareholders have been issued with 10 vouchers which will give a £1 discount on purchases totalling over £5 (excluding medicines, maps, books and gift vouchers) made in the Group's UK retail stores.

Shoes

STYLO *All Shareholders*
Every shareholder is entitled to two 20 per cent discount vouchers for use at Stylo retail outlets, trading as "Barratt" and "Stylo Instep" which are issued with the Annual Reports and Accounts.

Sports

HAWTIN *All Shareholders*
Shareholders are entitled to preferred terms on Gul International products. Apply to the registered office for these; 01222–488961.

HI-TEC SPORTS plc *All Shareholders*
It is the policy of the company to give perks on a one off basis. The offers are made to shareholders with the company's reports. They recently offered half price tennis footwear and reduced prices on outdoor foowear for men and women. While these offers are now closed, they have now introduced a further offer giving half price tennis shoes.

TOTTENHAM HOTSPUR plc *All shareholders*
10 per cent discount on purchases from Spurs Superstores and mail order purchases.

Stores

N. BROWN GROUP *All Shareholders*
Shareholders, subject to certain conditions are entitled to a 20 per cent discount only on purchases from any of the group's catalogues. Discounts are also available on a range of financial services via Morfitt and Turnbull.

STOREHOUSE plc *500 ordinary*
Shareholders are offered 10 per cent discount on purchases at the group's UK stores of up to £500 worth of merchandise. The discount is offered through vouchers which are dispatched with the Company Report and Accounts in June. They give 4 × £1 off when you spend £10 or more, 2 × £3 off when you spend £30 or more 8 × £5 off when you spend £50 or more. The vouchers are valid until 31 December. The company's stores include Bhs, Mothercare & Blazer.

TOYE & CO *250 ordinary*
Discounts of up to 25 per cent are available to shareholders as follows: 15 per cent discount for cash/cheque payments, 10 per cent credit card, off normal retail selling price on purchase of stock lines at retail shops of Toye, Kenning & Spencer Ltd in London, Bedworth, Glasgow, Preston, and Manchester. Discount also applies on orders sent through the post. 25 per cent discount for cash/cheque payments, 20 per cent credit card on Jewellery, Watches, Clocks, Cutlery, Glass, Silver Plate, Pewter,

Giftware, Sports Medals, Trophies, and Awards purchased over the counter only at John Taylor, Poston & Company showroom at 19–21 Great Queen St, London WC2B 5BE. Qualifying shareholders may apply for the shareholder's Special Purchase Card. This is available on request, from the date the member's name is entered on the Register. Upon its presentation at the time of purchase or the quotation of its serial number on postal orders the discount will be allowed. The discount may not be added to any other form of discount.

Telecommunications

BT *All Shareholders*

Shareholders are occasionally given limited period opportunities to buy BT products at a discount on the normal retail price. The decision whether or not to make any further offers is made on an ongoing basis, and details of any offers are usually given in the "Report to our Shareholders" sent with the interim and final dividend payments.

Travel

AIRTOURS *All Shareholders*

Shareholders are entitled to a 10 per cent discount on Airtours holidays booked through a special Shareholders' holiday advice line – telephone number 01706–232827. This offer relates to any holiday taken from any Airtours brochures including Tradewinds, Sun Express, Cruising and the Eurosites Camping brochure. Shareholders will need to quote their name and shareholder number as shown on their share certificate.

BARR & WALLACE ARNOLD TRUST *500 shares*

Shareholders are entitled to the following discounts: 15 per cent off Wallace Arnold holidays booked through a Wallace Arnold Travel Shop. 15 per cent off at any of the group's five hotels. Discounts on new cars; Vauxhall, Ford and Peugot. If shareholders wish to take up these offers they should contact Company Secretary; Mr Bell 0113–249 9332, who will issue a shareholder's concessionary card.

BRITISH AIRWAYS *200 ordinary as of 3/11/95*

A discount coupon is issued to shareholders which entitles the bearer and up to three additional family members, booking and travelling with them, to cut 10 per cent off the price of any published British Airways fare, subject to the normal terms and conditions. An additional coupon may be used to reduce by 5 per cent the basic price of any holiday from the British Airways holiday range. The coupon may only be used towards leisure travel, but it does offer a reduction on fares in any British Airways class of travel worldwide. The definition of a published fare is any fare listed in British Airways "Fares Fortnightly" tariff booklet. A special shareholder telephone number is issued for booking flights and buying tickets. 01345–600710.

ISLE OF MAN STEAM PACKET *2,000 to 12,000. Shareholders must be on the Register by the end of March to get perks for that year*

Shareholders are entitled to tickets for a return journey at half the approximate rate as follows: 2,000 to 3,999 shares: 1 passenger ticket. 4,000 to 7,999 2 passenger tickets. 8,000 to 11,999 3 passenger tickets. 12,000 + 3 passenger tickets and one car ticket. The concessionary tickets are available on Tariff C, D and E sailings. Tickets must be booked direct from the Head Office.

P & O *Varying amounts of Concessionary stock to qualify for discounts*

1. Min shareholding : 600 (600) 5.5 per cent £1 red. non-cum preferred concessionary stock. 50 per cent discount Dover–Calais, Felixstowe–Zeebrugge, 25 per cent discount Cairnyman–Larne, 40 per cent discount Portsmouth–Cherbourg, Portsmouth–Le Havre, Portsmouth–Bilbao, (this route is at the directors discretion and is not part of the scheme rules). 2. Min shareholding – 300 (nominal) 5.5 per cent £1 red non-cum preferred concessionary stock. Half the above discounts. Shareholders must be on the register on 31 December 1995, and at the time of travel, to qualify for discounted travel in 1996. The shareholder must travel personally and take a car, motorcycle, motorcaravan. They may be accompanied by up to three additional adults, two

children count as one adult. Concessionary bookings must be for return (two way) travel. Only individual stockholders can be eligible for fare discounts – no company or other corporate body or stock held in nominee accounts is eligible.

THE RANK ORGANISATION *All ordinary shareholders if held for 2 years or more*
A discount of 15 per cent will be available from 1st April 1996 until 31st March 1997 and can be used as part payment towards holidays booked from the following brochures; Butlins, Haven, Warner and Shearings. The shareholder must be included in the bookings, and booking must be made directly with Rank. The format of the shareholder perk after March 1997 will be communicated to shareholders with the annual report which will be published on or about 15th March 1997.

STANDARD CHARTERED *All shareholders*
Shareholders have been offered commission free travellers cheques.

TRAFALGAR HOUSE *1,000 ordinary and/or Convertible Cumulative Pref shares*
The discount applies to the shareholder and members of their party sharing their hotel room or travelling in the same cabin on Cunard holidays. Available for 1996 calendar year the discount applies to the full current published tariff in Cunard's main brochures for 1996, and cannot be combined with any other special offers. Shareholders are entitled to the following discounts : QE2 : any arrangement featuring Concorde, World Cruise, QE2 America holidays 10 per cent. QE2 cruises; one-way excursion and Air/Sea arrangements not excluded by above 15 per cent. Sagafjord-Vistafjord : Sagafjord World Cruise & any of its sectors. Sagafjord & Vistafjord holidays inc land tour/hotel stay 10 per cent. Sagafjord & Vistafjord cruises & fly/cruises 15 per cent. Sea Goddess I & II : Cruise and stay, cruise and tour holidays 10 per cent. Cruise and fly/cruises 15 per cent. Cunard Crown : cruise and stay holidays 10 per cent. Cruise and fly/cruises 15 per cent. River Cruises Cruises and fly/cruises 15 per cent. Cunard Hotels : Full room only tariff 15 per cent.

Wines and Spirits
DEVENISH plc
Last year shareholders were sent dining vouchers which entitled the shareholder to two free meals, excluding drinks, of starter, main course, and sweet at participating Devenish restaurants. The decision as to whether or not to repeat the offer this year has not been made yet.

ELDRIDGE, POPE & CO *All Shareholders*
Shareholders are offered discounts against purchases from Eldridge Pope wine shops. Meal discount vouchers are also available for use at selected pubs.

FULLER, SMITH & TURNER *£100 equivalent of nominal stock*
Shareholders owning more than £100 equivalent of nominal stock can buy beer, wine and spirits at preferential wholesale prices, including free delivery in the UK mainland. Payment is by credit card only. For full details please contact Lewis Ragbourn, Free Trade Sales Manager, telephone 0181–9662000.

GREENE KING *All Shareholders*
Each year shareholders are invited to take part in a discounted case of wine offer. Various wines are offered each year with a discount of 15–20 per cent on normal retail prices.

MERRYDOWN WINE *All Shareholders*
Exclusive terms are offered to shareholders on the price of Merrydown ciders and adult soft drinks. These must be purchased per case and a delivery charge is added to the price, but it is substantially reduced for shareholders. Shareholders with more than 215 shares are able to bring a guest to the Annual General Meeting and stay on for a drink and finger buffet after the meeting to meet the management.

SCOTTISH & NEWCASTLE *All Shareholders*
Details of the benefits offered to shareholders are mailed with the Annual Report & Accounts in July. The offer situation is reviewed annually. At present

shareholders are offered a discount of approximately 30 per cent on a maximum of four cases of selected wines and spirits from Waverley Vintners. The offer remains open for about 12 weeks. Secondly, there is the Premier Club Card Offer which offers a 10 per cent discount on meals, drinks taken with meals and accommodation in a special selection of about 500 establishments within the Retail Division. These include Homespreads, Country Carveries, Country Grills, S&N Hotels, Lodge Inns, Old Orleans and restaurant premises.

WHITBREAD *All Shareholders*

For the 1994/95 financial year only shareholders have received, with the Annual Report and Accounts, discount coupons representing a £43.50 discount when redeemed against total purchases of £290. The discount coupons can be used in virtually all of the company's retail outlets. The coupons may not be used in conjunction with any other offer and are not transferable. In addition the company offers a 12.5 per cent discount on Leisure Vouchers. This has increased from the 10 per cent discount offered last year. In addition this year there are two offers from the Country Club Hotel Group (part of Whitbread PLC). 1) Two vouchers for 15 per cent against brochure price of a Country Club Hotel Leisure or Gold Break booking. Valid until 31st October 1996. 2) A "3 night for the price of 2" offer is also available at selected hotels. This is available until the end of February 1997. This offer may be available at selected periods to non-shareholders.

Reprinted by courtesy of Hargreaves Lansdown Stockbrokers, Embassy House, Queen's Avenue, Clifton, Bristol BS8 1SB. Tel: 0117–988 9880.

Appendix 2

Recent Issues of National Savings Certificates

All the following issues are within the first five years of their life when fixed interest rates (pitched at a competitive level when the issue first goes on sale) apply. Thereafter variable interest is added every three months (see the general extension rate).

The compound rate of interest over the first five years is usually quoted. It is a useful yardstick for making long-term (i.e. five years in this case) comparisons.

As interest payments are not constant but increase towards the end of the term, check both the annual yield and the average return obtained from holding from now until the end of the term for more immediate comparisons.

Once these certificates reach the end of the five year term, variable interest is added every three months – known as the *general extension rate*. This is now below the compound rate of interest on the current issue of certificates and varies. The fixed interest rate extensions to older issues of certificates has been phased out and completely replaced by the general extension rate.

As interest is added either at three-monthly intervals (or four-monthly with older issues) when you cash in your certificates, do so immediately after a payment date. Check the purchase date on the certificates to calculate the interim anniversary dates.

Capital Bonds are not strictly speaking National Savings Certificates, because the interest is not tax free. It is accumulated before deduction of tax which has to be paid annually. However, their format is sufficiently similar to National Savings Certificates to include them in this detailed schedule of rates and values.

APPENDIX 2

36th Issue
Sold at £25 a unit from 2 April 1991 – 2 May 1992
Compound interest rate over first five years = 8.5%

Year	Interest: 3 monthly £	Value anniversary of purchase £	Yield anniversary of purchase %	Average yield to end term %
5	0.89¼	37.59	12.6	12.6

37th Issue
Sold at £25 a unit from 13 May 1992 – 5 August 1992
Compound interest rate over first five years = 8%

Year	Interest: 3 monthly £	Value anniversary of purchase £	Yield anniversary of purchase %	Average yield to end term %
5	0.91	36.74	11.0	11.0

38th Issue
Sold at £25 a unit from 24 August 1992 – 22 September 1992
(38th Reinvestment Issue from 6 August 1992 – 4 October 1992)
Compound interest rate over first five years = 7.5%

Year	Interest: 3 monthly £	Value anniversary of purchase £	Yield anniversary of purchase %	Average yield to end term %
5	0.85½	35.89	10.5	10.5

39th Issue
Sold at £100 a unit from 5 October 1992 – 12 November 1992
Compound interest rate over first five years = 6.75%

Year	Interest: 3 monthly £	Value anniversary of purchase £	Yield anniversary of purchase %	Average yield to end term %
5	2.95½	138.62	9.3	9.3

APPENDIX 2

40th Issue
Sold at £25 a unit from 7 December 1992 – 16 December 1993
(40th Reinvestment Issue from 13 November 1992)
Compound interest rate over first five years = 5.75%

Year	Interest: 3 monthly £	Value anniversary of purchase £	Yield anniversary of purchase %	Average yield to end term %
4	0.48½	30.64	6.8	7.3
5	0.60½	33.06	7.9	7.9

41st Issue
Sold at £25 a unit from 17 December 1993 – 19 September 1994
Compound interest rate over first five years = 5.4%

Year	Interest: 3 monthly £	Value anniversary of purchase £	Yield anniversary of purchase %	Average yield to end term %
3	0.3640	28.42	5.40	6.44
4	0.4547	30.24	6.40	6.97
5	0.5707	32.52	7.55	7.55

42nd Issue
Sold at £100 a unit from 20 September 1994 – 25 January 1996
Compound interest rate over first five years = 5.85%

Year	Interest: 3 monthly £	Value anniversary of purchase £	Yield anniversary of purchase %	Average yield to end term %
2	1.19½	108.78	4.6	6.32
3	1.49½	114.77	5.5	6.90
4	1.93½	122.51	6.75	7.60
5	2.59	132.88	8.46	8.46

43rd Issue
Sold at £100 a unit from 26 January 1996–
Compound interest rate over first five years = 5.35%

Year	Interest: 3 monthly £	Value anniversary of purchase £	Yield anniversary of purchase %	Average yield to end term %
1	3.75*	103.75	3.75	5.35
2	1.08	108.06	4.15	5.75
3	1.35	113.46	5.00	6.29
4	1.74	120.44	6.15	6.95
5	2.33	129.77	7.75	7.75

* Credited at end of first year.

8th Index-Linked Issue
Sold at £100 a unit from 20 September 1994 – 25 January 1996
Compound interest rate over first five years = 3.0% + Index-linking

Year	Value Anniversary of Purchase £	Extra Interest Yield Anniversary of Purchase
1	The value of your Certificate will	1.25% of purchase price
2	move in line with the rate of	1.75% of 1st anniversary value
3	inflation as measured by the RPI.	2.50% of 2nd anniversary value
4		3.50% of 3rd anniversary value
5		6.07% of 4th anniversary value

9th Index-Linked Issue
Sold at £100 a unit from 26 January 1996–
Compound interest rate over first five years = 2.5% + Index-linking

Year	Value Anniversary of Purchase £	Extra Interest Yield Anniversary of Purchase
1	The value of your Certificate will	1.0% of purchase price
2	move in line with the rate of	1.25% of 1st anniversary value
3	inflation as measured by the RPI.	2.0% of 2nd anniversary value
4		3.0% of 3rd anniversary value
5		5.31% of 4th anniversary value

APPENDIX 2

Capital Bond Series "C"
Sold at £100 a unit from 2 April 1991 – 2 May 1992
Gross compound interest rate over first five years = 11.5%

Year	Annual gross interest £	Value anniversary of purchase £	Gross yield anniversary of purchase %	Net[1] %	Gross average yield to end term %	Net[1] %
5	25.42	172.34	17.3	13.0	17.3	13.0

Capital Bond Series "D"
Sold at £100 a unit from 13 May 1992 – 5 August 1992
Gross compound interest rate over first five years = 10.75%

Year	Annual gross interest £	Value anniversary of purchase £	Gross yield anniversary of purchase %	Net[1] %	Gross average yield to end term %	Net[1] %
5	23.94	166.62	16.8	12.5	16.7	10.6

Capital Bond Series "E"
Sold at £100 a unit from 24 August 1992 – 22 September 1992
Gross compound interest rate over five years = 10%

Year	Annual gross interest £	Value anniversary of purchase £	Gross yield anniversary of purchase %	Net[1] %	Gross average yield to end term %	Net[1] %
5	19.96	161.05	14.2	10.6	14.2	10.6

Capital Bond Series "F"
Sold at £100 a unit from 5 October 1992 – 12 November 1992
Gross compound interest rate over five years = 9%

Year	Annual gross interest £	Value anniversary of purchase £	Gross yield anniversary of purchase %	Net[1] %	Gross average yield to end term %	Net[1] %
5	17.16	153.90	12.6	9.4	12.6	9.4

[1] Net of 25% tax.

APPENDIX 2

Capital Bond Series "G"
Sold at £100 a unit from 7 December 1992 – 16 December 1993
Gross compound interest rate over five years = 7.75%

Year	Annual gross interest £	Value anniversary of purchase £	Gross yield anniversary of purchase %	Net[1] yield anniversary of purchase %	Gross average yield to end term %	Net[1] average yield to end term %
4	10.80	130.90	9.0	6.8	9.9	7.5
5	14.33	145.23	11.0	8.2	11.0	8.2

Capital Bond Series "H"
Sold at £100 a unit from 17 December 1993 – 19 September 1994
Gross compound interest rate over five years = 7%

Year	Annual gross interest £	Value anniversary of purchase £	Gross yield anniversary of purchase %	Net[1] yield anniversary of purchase %	Gross average yield to end term %	Net[1] average yield to end term %
3	8.07	118.69	7.30	5.48	8.66	6.49
4	9.97	128.66	8.40	6.30	9.34	7.01
5	13.24	141.90	10.29	7.72	10.29	7.72

Capital Bond Series "I"
Sold at £100 a unit from 20 September 1994 – 25 Janaury 1996
Gross compound interest rate over five years = 7.75%

Year	Annual gross interest £	Value anniversary of purchase £	Gross yield anniversary of purchase %	Net[1] yield anniversary of purchase %	Gross average yield to end term %	Net[1] average yield to end term %
2	6.41	111.56	6.1	4.58	8.41	6.31
3	8.48	120.04	7.6	5.70	9.19	6.89
4	10.81	130.85	9.0	6.75	10.00	7.50
5	14.39	145.24	11.0	8.25	11.00	8.25

[1] Net of 25% tax.

APPENDIX 2

Capital Bond Series "J"
Sold at £100 a unit from 26 January 1996
Gross compound interest rate over five years = 6.65%

Year	Annual gross interest £	Value anniversary of purchase £	Gross yield anniversary of purchase %	Net* anniversary of purchase %	Gross average yield to end term %	Net* yield to end term %
2	5.44	110.04	5.2	4.16	7.17	5.74
3	6.71	116.75	6.1	4.88	7.84	6.27
4	9.02	125.77	7.7	6.18	8.71	6.97
5	12.21	137.98	9.6	7.76	9.70	7.76

* Assuming tax paid at 20% savings rate.

Children's Bonus Bond
Sold at £25 a unit

Issue on sale	Interest p.a. 1st four years %	Bonus 5th anniversary %	Yield 5th anniversary %	Value of £25 unit 5th anniversary £
Issue "A" 8/7/91 – 2/5/92	5.0	47.36	11.84	43.75
Issue "B" 23/5/92 – 5/8/92	5.0	40.12	10.90	41.94
Issue "C" 24/8/92 – 22/9/92	5.0	34.16	10.10	40.45
Issue "D" 5/10/92 – 12/11/92	5.0	26.96	9.10	38.65
Issue "E" 7/12/92 – 16/12/93	5.0	18.28	7.85	36.48
Issue "F" 17/12/93 – 19/9/94	5.0	14.92	7.35	35.64
Issue "G" 20/9/94 – 25/1/96	5.0	18.28	7.85	36.48
Issue "H" 26/1/96	5.0	11.00	6.75	34.66

APPENDIX 2

FIRST Option Bond
Sold at £1,000 minimum

Issue on sale	Guaranteed rate first 12 months** gross %	net* %	Bonus on £20,000 plus gross %	net* %
7/7/92–21/7/92 (12 noon)	10.34	7.75	0.4	0.3
21/7/92–4/10/92 (12 noon)	9.67	7.25	0.4	0.3
5/10/92–12/11/92	8.67	6.50	0.4	0.3
22/3/93–16/12/93	6.34	4.75	0.4	0.3
17/12/93–19/9/94	6.00	4.50	0.4	0.3
20/9/94–25/1/96	6.4	4.8	0.4	0.3
26/1/96	6.25	5.0‡	0.25	0.2‡

Pensioners Guaranteed Income Bond
Sold at £500 minimum

Issue on sale	Interest Rate fixed for 5 years gross %	net* %
Series "1" 21/1/94–19/9/94	7.00	5.25
Series "2" 20/9/94–25/1/96	7.50	5.63
Series "3" 26/1/91	7.0	5.6‡

Capital Bond Series "A"–"I"
Interest is added at the end of each twelve months.
* Net of basic rate tax at 25%. From 1996 rates are net of 20% tax.
** FIRST Option Bond: anniversary interest for the next twelve months at the current guaranteed rate.
‡ Net of 20% rate tax.

177

APPENDIX 2

General Extension Rates: Interest Variable

After the fixed term ends, interest, at the GER, is added every three months, although interest is calculated monthly at the rate in force at the beginning of each month.

17 June 1982 to 30 November 1982 8.4%
1 December 1982 to 31 August 1983 7.08%
1 September 1983 to 31 March 1984 7.68%
1 April 1984 to 31 July 1984 6.84%
1 August 1984 to 30 November 1984 8.52%
1 December 1984 to 31 January 1985 8.28%
1 February 1985 to 31 March 1985 9%
1 April 1985 to 30 September 1985 9.51%
1 October 1985 to 31 October 1986 8.01%
1 November 1986 to 31 March 1987 8.7%
1 April 1987 to 31 April 1987 7.5%
1 May 1987 to 30 September 1987 7.02%
1 October 1987 to 29 February 1988 6.51%
1 March 1988 to 30 April 1988 5.76%
1 May 1988 to 30 November 1992 5.01%
1 December 1992 to 31 December 1993 3.75%
1 January 1994 3.51%

The current rate can be obtained at your local post office, by phoning 0171–605 9461 or looking on Prestel page 5004213. The following Ansaphone numbers will also provide the current rate:
South – London – 0171–605 9483/9484
North – Lytham St Anne's – 01253 723714
Scotland – Glasgow – 0141–632 2766

Older Issues of National Savings Certificates

1st to 6th Issues
Sold between February 1916 and November 1939

Sell immediately. They yield between 1.2% and 2% a year.

Decimal, 7th, 8th, 9th, 10th, 11th, 12th, 14th, 16th, 18th, 19th, 21st, 23rd, 24th, 25th, 26th, 27th, 28th, 29th, 30th, 31st, 32nd, 33rd, 34th and 35th.
All units now earn variable General Extension Rate interest every 3 months; currently 3.51%

There were no 13th, 15th, 17th, 20th and 22nd Issues

Appendix 3

The Retail Prices Index

The Retail Prices Index is the official measure of inflation or the cost of living. On the second Tuesday of each month about 300–400 employees from benefit offices around the country check the prices of over 600 goods and services purchased by typical families. These are collated by the Department of Employment and issued as an index number released on the second or third Friday of the following month. The index was re-based in January 1987 to take account of changes in our shopping habits, so all subsequent index numbers will appear lower than those listed on page **180**, which have not been adjusted for the change.

Index-Linked Savings Certificates

When you buy National Savings Index-Linked Certificates the index number which is used to work out the subsequent rise in the value of your certificates is the one for two months earlier. If you buy certificates in June, it is the April index number – which is published in May – which is the starting base.

When you encash your certificate, the same rules apply. The cash-in value of your certificates in June will relate to the April index-linked value, published in May.

On the Wednesday following publication of the RPI, *Money Mail* gives the latest value of certificates if they are sold the *next* month. As eight working days' notice is required, the following month is the earliest date at which the certificates can be encashed.

APPENDIX 3

UK Retail Prices Index – 1981 to 1996

	1981	1982	1983	1984	1985	1986	1987	1988
Average	295.0	320.4	335.1	351.7	373.2	385.9	101.9	106.3
Jan	277.3	310.6	325.9	342.6	359.8	379.7	100.0	103.3
Feb	279.8	310.7	327.3	344.0	362.7	381.1	100.4	103.3
March	284.0	313.4	327.9	345.1	366.1	381.6	100.6	103.7
April	292.2	319.7	332.5	349.7	373.9	385.3	101.8	104.1
May	294.1	322.0	333.9	351.0	375.6	386.0	101.9	105.8
June	295.8	322.9	334.7	351.9	376.4	385.8	101.9	106.2
July	297.1	323.0	336.5	351.5	375.7	384.7	101.8	106.6
Aug	299.3	323.1	338.0	354.8	376.7	385.9	102.1	106.7
Sept	301.0	322.9	339.5	355.5	376.5	387.8	102.4	107.9
Oct	303.7	324.5	340.7	357.7	377.1	388.4	102.9	108.4
Nov	306.9	326.1	341.9	358.8	378.4	391.7	103.4	109.5
Dec	308.8	325.5	342.8	358.5	378.9	393.0	103.3	110.0

	1989	1990	1991	1992	1993	1994	1995	1996
Average	115.2	126.1	133.5	138.5	140.7	144.1	149.1	152.7
Jan	111.0	119.5	130.2	135.6	137.9	141.3	146.0	150.2
Feb	111.8	120.2	130.9	136.3	138.8	142.1	146.9	150.9
March	112.3	121.4	131.4	136.7	139.3	142.5	147.5	151.5
April	114.3	125.1	133.1	138.8	140.6	144.2	149.0	152.6
May	115.0	126.2	133.5	139.3	141.1	144.7	149.6	152.9
June	115.4	126.7	134.1	139.3	141.0	144.7	149.8	153.0
July	115.5	126.8	133.8	138.8	140.7	144.0	149.1	152.4
Aug	115.8	128.1	134.1	138.9	141.3	144.7	149.9	153.1
Sept	116.6	129.3	134.6	139.4	141.9	145.0	150.6	153.8
Oct	117.5	130.3	135.1	139.9	141.8	145.2	149.8	153.8
Nov	118.5	130.0	135.6	139.7	141.6	145.3	149.8	153.9
Dec	118.8	129.9	135.7	139.2	141.9	146.0	150.7	154.4

Index rebased January 1987 = 100. Divide "old" index numbers by 3.945 to convert to new base.

Source: Central Statistics Office. For earlier or later numbers phone 0171–533 5874

Appendix 4

CAR: The Real Rate of Interest

The flat investment interest rates quoted by banks and building societies are sometimes followed by a slightly higher rate and the letters CAR. This stands for "compound annual rate".

If you reinvest your income in the same account, rather than spend it, it can affect the real rate of interest you receive. Interest paid more frequently than once a year and reinvested itself begins to earn interest. And interest on interest adds up to a slightly higher interest rate than the flat quoted rate.

The compound effect of interest paid at intervals ranging from monthly to annually can add up to useful extra interest on larger investments, particularly when interest rates in general are high. If you spend your income, only the flat rate is relevant.

Compounded Annual Interest Rates

Quoted rate* %	Annually %	Half-yearly %	Quarterly %	Monthly %
5.00	5.00	5.06	5.09	5.12
5.50	5.50	5.58	5.61	5.64
6.00	6.00	6.09	6.14	6.17
6.50	6.50	6.61	6.66	6.70
7.00	7.00	7.12	7.19	7.23
7.50	7.50	7.64	7.71	7.76
8.00	8.00	8.16	8.24	8.30
8.50	8.50	8.68	8.77	8.84
9.00	9.00	9.20	9.31	9.38
9.50	9.50	9.73	9.84	9.92
10.00	10.00	10.25	10.38	10.47
10.50	10.50	10.78	10.92	11.02
11.00	11.00	11.30	11.46	11.57
11.50	11.50	11.83	12.01	12.13
12.00	12.00	12.36	12.55	12.68
12.50	12.50	12.89	13.10	13.24
13.00	13.00	13.42	13.65	13.80
13.50	13.50	13.96	14.20	14.37
14.00	14.00	14.49	14.75	14.93
14.50	14.50	15.03	15.31	15.50
15.00	15.00	15.56	15.87	16.08

* Net rate. Interest is taxable even if it is reinvested, so taxpayers cannot benefit in full from the compound gross interest.

APPENDIX 4

Gross and Net Interest Rates

Banks and building societies quote savings rates without deduction of tax. Use the tables below to find out the net rate. Interest paid to taxpayers has 20 per cent deducted at source; higher rate taxpayers must pay the difference between 20 per cent and the higher rate tax of 40 per cent.

Interest rates after tax			Interest rates after tax			Interest rates after tax		
Gross rate%	Net of 20%	Net of 40%	Gross rate%	Net of 20%	Net of 40%	Gross rate%	Net of 20%	Net of 40%
2.00	1.60	1.20	3.85	3.08	2.31	5.70	4.56	3.42
2.05	1.64	1.23	3.90	3.12	2.34	5.75	4.60	3.45
2.10	1.68	1.26	3.95	3.16	2.37	5.80	4.64	3.48
2.15	1.72	1.29	4.00	3.20	2.40	5.85	4.68	3.51
2.20	1.76	1.32	4.05	3.24	2.43	5.90	4.72	3.54
2.25	1.80	1.35	4.10	3.28	2.46	5.95	4.76	3.57
2.30	1.84	1.38	4.15	3.32	2.49	6.00	4.80	3.60
2.35	1.88	1.41	4.20	3.36	2.52	6.05	4.84	3.63
2.40	1.92	1.44	4.25	3.40	2.55	6.10	4.88	3.66
2.45	1.96	1.47	4.30	3.44	2.58	6.15	4.92	3.69
2.50	2.00	1.50	4.35	3.48	2.61	6.20	4.96	3.72
2.55	2.04	1.53	4.40	3.52	2.64	6.25	5.00	3.75
2.60	2.08	1.56	4.45	3.56	2.67	6.30	5.04	3.78
2.65	2.12	1.59	4.50	3.60	2.70	6.35	5.08	3.81
2.70	2.16	1.62	4.55	3.64	2.73	6.40	5.12	3.84
2.75	2.20	1.65	4.60	3.68	2.76	6.45	5.16	3.87
2.80	2.24	1.68	4.65	3.72	2.79	6.50	5.20	3.90
2.85	2.28	1.71	4.70	3.76	2.82	6.55	5.24	3.93
2.90	2.32	1.74	4.75	3.80	2.85	6.60	5.28	3.96
2.95	2.36	1.77	4.80	3.84	2.88	6.65	5.32	3.99
3.00	2.40	1.80	4.85	3.88	2.91	6.70	5.36	4.02
3.05	2.44	1.83	4.90	3.92	2.94	6.75	5.40	4.05
3.10	2.48	1.86	4.95	3.96	2.97	6.80	5.44	4.08
3.15	2.52	1.89	5.00	4.00	3.00	6.85	5.48	4.11
3.20	2.56	1.92	5.05	4.04	3.03	6.90	5.52	4.14
3.25	2.60	1.95	5.10	4.08	3.06	6.95	5.56	4.17
3.30	2.64	1.98	5.15	4.12	3.09	7.00	5.60	4.20
3.35	2.68	2.01	5.20	4.16	3.12	7.05	5.64	4.23
3.40	2.72	2.04	5.25	4.20	3.15	7.10	5.68	4.26
3.45	2.76	2.07	5.30	4.24	3.18	7.15	5.72	4.29
3.50	2.80	2.10	5.35	4.28	3.21	7.20	5.76	4.32
3.55	2.84	2.13	5.40	4.32	3.24	7.25	5.80	4.35
3.60	2.88	2.16	5.45	4.36	3.27	7.30	5.84	4.38
3.65	2.92	2.19	5.50	4.40	3.30	7.35	5.88	4.41
3.70	2.96	2.22	5.55	4.44	3.33	7.40	5.92	4.44
3.75	3.00	2.25	5.60	4.48	3.36	7.45	5.96	4.47
3.80	3.04	2.28	5.65	4.52	3.39	7.50	6.00	4.50

Index

Accommodation, satisfaction with 2
Accumulation and maintenance trusts 15
Additional voluntary contributions 28, 124–5
Affording savings 1
Age allowance 21, 31
Allowances tax 12, 14, 24, 25, 30
  age 21, 31
Annuities
  flexible 76–7
  pension 7, 23, 74–5
  purchased 31, 73–4
  self-employed retirement 23, 74–6, 127–9
  temporary 93–4
Assets, CGT exemptions 16–17
Assisted Places Scheme 29

'Back to backs' 93–4
Bank Deposit Protection Scheme 33
Banking Ombudsman 33
Banks 34–48
  children's account 34–5
  deposit account 35–6
  direct debits 7
  fixed term accounts 47–8
  high interest cheque account 36–8
  instant access accounts 38–9
  interest-bearing current accounts 39–40
  investment risk 9, 10
  investor protection 33
  monthly income accounts 40–1
  notice accounts 41–2
  overdraft interest 5–6
  Save As You Earn (SAYE) 43–5
  tax exempt special savings account 45–6
  tax on interest 20–1
Benefits, income tax on 13
Bond Funds 151–2

Bonds
  capital 99–100, 174–6
  children's bonus 101–2, 176
  deposit 102
  distribution 77–9
  FIRST option 98–9, 177
  funds 151–2
  guaranteed growth and income 79–80, 177
  guaranteed stock market (equity) 80–2
  income 79–80, 82–3, 103–4
  local authority 95–6
  managed 83–4
  negotiable 96–7
  pensioners guaranteed income 110–11, 177
  premium 111–12
  with-profits 92–3
  yearling 96–7
Bonus bonds, children's 101–2, 176
Budget planner 1, 3
British government see Government stock
Building societies 49–68
  cash card accounts 49–50
  children's account 52–3
  current account 50–1
  fixed term share 67–8
  high interest cheque accounts 55–6
  instant access accounts 53–5
  investment risk 10
  investor protection 33
  monthly income account 56–7
  notice account 57–9
  offshore savings account 115–16
  ordinary (share) account 59–60
  postal account 60–1
  regular savings account 62–3
  Save As You Earn (SAYE) 63–5
  tax exempt special savings account 66–7
  tax on interest 20–1

Buildings Societies Compensation Scheme 33
Buildings Societies Ombudsman 33
Business Expansion Scheme (BES) 17, 132

Capital Investment Categories 9–11
Capital bonds 99–100, 174–6
Capital gains tax (CGT) 16–17
Capital taxes 16–18
CAR (compound annual rate of interest) 181–2
Car companies, shareholder perks 158–9
Cars
  CGT exemption 17
  savings for 29
Cash card accounts
  banks 38–9
  building societies 49–50
CGT (capital gains tax) 16–17
Chattels, CGT exemption 17
Cheque accounts
  banks 36–8, 118–19
  building societies 49–51, 55–6
Children
  bank accounts 34–5
  bonus bonds 101–2, 176
  building society account 52–3
  savings for 25
  school fees 29–30, 85–6
Cluster policies 90
Coins, gold 69–70
Commodities, investment risk 11
Company loans 8
Compensation schemes 33
Compound annual rate of interest (CAR) 181
Confectionery Companies, shareholder perks 159
Consolidation loans 8
Credit, interest-free 8

183

INDEX

Currency, investment risk 11
Currency funds 117–18
  managed 119–20
Current accounts
  banks 36–8, 39–40, 118–19
  building societies 49–51, 55–6

DIY companies, shareholder perks 159
Death
  financial protection of family 2
  gifts made within seven years of 18
Debenture stock 156–7
Deposit accounts
  banks 35–6
  building societies 53
Deposit bonds 102
Deposit takers
  investment risk 9, 10
  tax on interest 20–1
Direct debits 4, 7
Disability, financial protection of family 2, 27
Discretionary trusts 15
Distribution bonds 77–9
Dividend income 22
Divorce, savings strategies 30
Dry cleaning companies, shareholder perks 159–60

Education, school fees 29–30, 85–6
EIS (Enterprise Investment Scheme) 17, 132–4
Elderly people *see* Pensions; Retirement
Electricity companies, direct debit savings 4
Emergency savings 2, 26–7
Employees, saving for retirement 28
Endowment policies 2
  traded (second hand) 4, 86–7
  with-profits 89–90
Enterprise Investment Scheme (EIS) 17, 132–4
Equipment, rented 8
Equity bonds 80–2
Escalator bonds 47, 67
Essential savings 2, 26–8
  emergencies 26–7
  financial protection for family 27
  house 27–8
  retirement 28
Exempt assets, CGT 16–17
Exempt gifts, IHT 18

Families 24–5
  financial protection 2, 27
Fashion companies, shareholder perks 160–1
Financial protection for family 2, 27
Financial Services Act 1986 32–3

Financial services companies, shareholder perks 161
FIRST option bonds 98–9, 177
Fixed capital investment risks 9–10
Fixed interest investment risks 9–10
Fixed rate term accounts 121–2
Fixed term accounts 47–8
Fixed term shares 67–8
Flexible annuities 76–7
Flexible policies, with profits 90–1
Food companies, shareholder perks 161
43rd issue savings certificates 109–10, 173
Free-standing AVCs 28, 124–5
Friendly societies 71–2
Furnishing companies, shareholder perks 161–2

General Extension Rates (GER) 178
Gifts
  parental 25
  tax on 15, 17, 18
Gilt-edged securities *see* Government stock
'Gold' cards 6
Gold coins 69–70
Government stock 17, 154–6
  index-linked 152–4
  tax on interest 21–2
Granny bonds 107–8
Grants, income tax 13
Gross and Net interest rates 182
Grossing up tax paid interest 21
Guaranteed growth bonds 79–80
Guaranteed income bonds 79–80
  pensioners 110–11, 177
Guaranteed stock market bonds 80–2

Health companies, shareholder perks 162
High income bonds 82–3
High interest cheque accounts
  banks 36–8
  building societies 55–6
  offshore savings 118–19
Holidays, saving for 29
Home income plans 31
  CGT exemption 16–17
  saving for 27–8
Hotel companies, shareholder perks 162–3
Houses *see* Homes
Husbands and wives, taxation 24–5

IFA Promotion 30
IHT (inheritance tax) 15, 17–18
IMRO (Investment Managers Regulatory Organisation) 33
Income bonds 103–4
  guaranteed 79–80, 110–11, 177
  high 82–3

Income tax 12–15
  See also Allowances
Independent Schools Information Service 29
Index-linked savings certificates 107–8, 179
Index-linked government stock 152–4
Indexation, capital gains 17
Inheritance tax (IHT) 15, 17–18
Inland Revenue
  free tax leaflets 19
  notification of interest 21
Instant access accounts
  banks 38–9
  building societies 53–5
Insurance Ombudsman 33
Interest
  compound annual rate (CAR) 181–2
  current accounts with 36–8, 39–40
  General Extension Rate 178
  grossing up 'tax paid' 21
  Inland Revenue check 21
  investment categories 9–11
  National Savings accounts 21–2, 170
  overdraft 5–6
  tax on 20–2
Interest-free credit 8
Interest in possession trusts 15
Investment accounts 104–5
Investment categories 9–11
Investment funds 122–3
Investment trusts 134–5
  investment risk 11
  PEP 146–7
  savings scheme 135–6
Investor protection 32–3

Jewellery companies, shareholder perks 163

LAUTRO 32
Leaflets, free tax 19
Legal tender, CGT exemption 17
Life assurance *see* Life insurance
Life insurance 2, 27, 73–94
  annuities 73–4
  CGT exemption 17
  distribution bonds 77–9
  flexible annuities 76–7
  guaranteed growth and income bonds 79–80
  guaranteed stock market bonds 80–2
  high income bonds 82–3
  investment risk 9, 10, 11
  managed bonds 83–5
  pension annuities 74–6
  school fees educational trust 85–6
  second-hand (traded) policies 4, 86–7
  tax treatment 22–3

INDEX

temporary annuities (back to backs) 93–4
unit linked regular savings plan 87–9
with-profits bonds 92–3
with-profits endowment policies 89–90
with-profits flexible policies 90–1
Living accommodation, satisfaction with 2
'Loan-back' arrangements 6
Loan stock 156–7
Loans
  company 8
  consolidation 8
  tax on interest 20–1
Local authorities 95–7
  bonds 95–6
  investment risk 10
  loan interest 20–1
  negotiables or yearling bonds 96–7
  tax on interest 20–1
Lump sum savings 26–7, 30

Maintenance payments 12, 30
Managed bonds 83–5
Managed currency fund 119–21
Married Couple's tax allowance 14, 24
Monthly income accounts
  banks 40–1
  building societies 56–7
Monthly outgoings *see* Outgoings per month
Mortgages 2, 12, 27–8

National Savings 20, 98–114
  CGT exemption 17
  capital bonds 99–100, 174–6
  children's bonus bonds 101–2, 176
  deposit bonds 102
  FIRST option bonds 98–9, 177
  general extension rates 178
  income bonds, 103–4
  index-linked savings certificates 107–8, 179
  investment accounts 104–5
  investment risk 10
  ordinary accounts 105–7
  pensioners guaranteed income bonds 110–11, 177
  premium bonds 111–12
  Save As You Earn (SAYE) 113–14
  savings certificates 109–10
    older issues 178
    recent issues 170–3
  tax on interest 21–2
  yearly plan 114
Negotiable bonds 96–7
Non-working widows 31
Non-working wives 24–5, 115, 116

Notice accounts
  banks 41–2
  building societies 57–59

Occupational Pensions Advisory Service 131
OEIC (Open Ended Investment Funds) 122
Offshore savings 115–23
  building society accounts 115–16
  currency funds 117–18
  fixed rate term accounts 121–2
  high interest cheque accounts 118–19
  investment funds 122–3
  investment risk 9, 10, 11
  managed currency funds 119–21
  tax on interest 21–2
Old people *see* Pensions; Retirement
Open Ended Investment Funds (OEIC) 122
Ombudsman 33, 131
Ordinary accounts
  building societies 59–60
  National Savings 105–7
Ordinary quoted shares 137–9
Outgoings per month
  desirable costs 7
  flexible costs 6
  important costs 5
  other essentials 4
  unavoidable expenditure 3
Overdraft interest 5–6

Parental gifts 25
Pension annuities 7, 23, 74–6
Pensioners guaranteed income bonds 110–11, 177
Pensions 2, 6–7, 28, 124–31
  additional voluntary contributions 28, 124–5
  income tax 12, 13
  investment risk 10
  Occupational Pensions Advisory Service 131
  self-employed retirement annuities 23, 74–6, 127–9
  transfer plans 129–30
  see also Personal pensions
Pensions Ombudsman 33, 131
PEP *see* Personal Equity Plans
Perks, shareholder 158–69
Permanent disability
  family financial protection of, 2, 27
Permanent health insurance 27
Permanent interest bearing shares 140–2
Personal allowances 14, 24, 25, 30
Personal Equity Plans (PEP) 139–40
  investment or unit trusts 146–7
  tax 17, 20

Personal Investment Authority (PIA) 33, 131
Personal pensions 28, 126–7
  tax treatment 23
Photography companies, shareholder perks 164
PIA (Personal Investment Authority) 33, 131
PIBS (Permanent Interest Bearing Shares) 140–2
Postal accounts, building societies 60–1
Premium bonds 20, 111–12
Principal home, CGT exemption 16–17
Property companies, shareholder perks 164–5
Protection of investors 32–3
Publishing companies, shareholder perks 165
Purchased annuities 31, 73–4

Rainy day savings 2
Ratings symbols 9
Reasons for saving 1–8
Redundancy, savings strategies 30
Regular savings accounts 27
  building society 62–3
  friendly society 71–2
  unit-linked 87–9
Rented equipment 8
Restaurants, shareholder perks 165
Retail Prices Index 17, 152, 179, 180
Retailing companies, shareholder perks 166–7
Retirement 2, 28, 31
  see also Pensions
Retirement annuities 23, 74–6, 127–9
Reversionary bonuses 89, 92
Risk
  categories 9–11
  investor protection 32–3

Save As You Earn (SAYE)
  banks 43–5
  building societies 63–5
  National Savings 113–14
  tax 20
Saving certificates 109–10, 170–3, 178
  index linked 107–8, 179
School fees 29–30
  educational trusts 85–6
Second-hand (traded) life assurance policies 4, 86–7
Section 226 policies 23
Securities and Investment Board (SIB) 32, 33
Securities and Futures Authority (SFA) 33
Self-employed retirement annuities 23, 28, 74–6, 127–9
7th issue index-linked certificates 107–9
SFA (Securities and Futures Authority) 33

185

INDEX

Share accounts, building societies 59–60
Shareholder perks 158–69
Share option schemes 113
Shares 132–50
   Business Expansion Scheme 132
   dividend income 22
   Enterprise Investment Scheme 132–5
   investment risk 10–11
   investment trusts 134–5
   investment or unit trust PEPs 146–7
   investment trust savings scheme 135–7
   ordinary quoted 137–9
   permanent interest bearing 140–2
   Personal Equity Plans 139–40
   unit trusts 143–5
   unit savings schemes 147–8
   Unlisted Securities Market 142–3
   venture capital trusts 148–50
Short-term savings 29
SIB (Securities and Investment Board) 32, 33
Spirit and wine companies, shareholder perks 168–9
Sports companies, shareholder perks 166
Stock market
   guaranteed bonds 80–2
   quoted shares 137–9, 140–1, 142–3
Stocks 10, 151–57
   bond funds 151–52
   loans and debentures 156–7
   see also Government stock
Stores companies, shareholder perks 166–7
Strategies for saving 29–31
   divorce 30
   lump sum investments 30
   redundancy 30
   retirement 31
   school fees 29–30
   short-term savings 29
   very old 31
   widowhood 30–1

Tangible movable property, CGT exemption 17
Tax credits 22
Tax Exempt Special Savings Accounts (TESSAs)
   banks 29, 45–6
   building societies 27, 29, 66–7
   tax 17, 20
Tax-free investments 20
Taxation 12–23
   capital gains tax 16–17
   income tax 12–15
   inheritance tax 15, 17–18
   Inland Revenue leaflets 19
   investment treatment 20–3
   tips 3, 5, 6, 7
   trust income 15
   working out tax bill 13
Telecommunications companies, shareholder perks 167
Temporary annuities 93–4
Term accounts
   banks 47–8
   offshore savings 121–2
Term shares, building societies 67–8
Terminal bonuses 89, 92
TESSAs *see* Tax Exempt Special Savings Accounts
Traded endowment policies 4, 86–7
Transfer plans, pensions 129–30
Travel companies, shareholder perks 167–8
Trusts
   investment 134–5, 135–6, 146–7
   school fees educational trusts 85–6
   tax 15
   venture capital 149–50
   See also Unit trusts

UCITS (Undertaking for Collective Investments in Transferable Securities) 122–3
Unemployment benefit 30
Unit trusts 143–5
   bond funds 151–2
   dividend income 22
   investment risk 11
   investor protection 33
   PEP 146–7
   savings scheme 147–8
Unit-linked regular savings plan 87–9
Unlisted Securities Market, shares quoted on 142–3

Variable capital investment 10–11
Variable currency investment 11
Variable interest investment 10–11
Venture capital trusts 148–50
Very old people 31

Weddings, saving for 29
Widowhood
   allowances 30
   savings strategies 30–1
Wine and spirit companies, shareholder perks 168–9
With-profits bonds 92–3
With-profits endowment policies 89–90
With-profits flexible policies 90–1
Wives, taxation 24–5
Working out tax bill 13

Yearling bonds, local authority 96–7